# Agile Pro

# Management

*The Ultimate Step by Step Guide. Discover Effective Agile Tools to Manage Projects and Productivity to Improve Your Business and Leadership.*

**Daniel Stevens**

ISBN: 978-1-80271-118-9

# Table of Contents

## Introduction

Agile project management is an repetitive approach to software development that guarantees that feedback is easily acted on and that improvements are made in a timely manner at each step of a sprint or product cycle. This enables project teams to use agile project management methodologies to complete tasks effectively and collaboratively while staying within a project's timeline and budget.

Agile project management encompasses a wide range of methodologies, many of which are based around a set of common agile concepts and ideals.

However, there is no one-size-fits-all "agile methodology." So, where did they all originate?

The majority of today's agile project management techniques find their origins in software development. In the 1990s, tech teams discovered that conventional project management methodologies (such as Waterfall) were just not cutting it when it came to the way they wanted to function. They were discovering that the drawbacks of these heavyweight approaches — such as a lack of versatility, adaptability, and even autonomy — made it more difficult for them to react to change and integrate their learning's while on the job. There was no place for surprises because the project plans were laid out from the start, and deviations could be expensive. However, unlike enterprises where the procedure was set and the result was predictable and steady (think about a production process that produces the same product on an assembly line), software projects need constant adjustment. Perhaps stakeholder requirements change or perhaps research shows that anything isn't running well until an end-user has it. Rather than being bound by the project management strategy they outlined at the outset, agile project management approaches enabled teams to take those improvements into account in order to provide the best available product. They required faster production cycles (known as sprints), a more iterative approach, and constant feedback and monitoring to accomplish this. Don't panic if this all sounds like it's about app production. Many agile project management methodologies were created with applications in mind. Still, the fundamental agile values and agile project management principles are applicable to a wide range of teams, including product and marketing teams. Knowing the history of agile project management (or at least the overview discussed above) will help put some of the terms and procedures that now describe agile project management into perspective. We'll go through in more depth as we break down the Agile Manifesto. Here's a useful agile project management definition if you're just looking for a definition of agile project management right now, rather than the backstory of what it used to be.

# Chapter 1 Project Management in an Agile Environment

Agile Project Management (APM) is a method for organizing and directing project operations that splits them down into smaller cycles such as sprints or iterations.

An Agile project is done in small parts, much like Agile software development. An iteration is a single development step in Agile Software Development, for example. The project committee should include members from the project's different stakeholders, reviews, and critiques each part or version. The insights obtained from an iteration's critique are used to decide what the project's next move should be.

The opportunity to adapt to problems when they emerge in the project is the biggest advantage of getting underway in Agile Project Management. Making a desired adjustment to a project at the right time will save time and money while still ensuring that the project is completed on time and on budget.

## What exactly is APM?

Agile project management divides tasks into small chunks that are completed in work sessions that span the original concept process to monitoring and quality assurance (QA). These sessions are often referred to as sprints, which is the term for iteration used in the Scrum Agile development process.

Sprints are usually short, lasting a few days or weeks; they usually last two or four weeks.

Teams may use the Agile approach to release segments when they are finished. This continuous release schedule enables teams to show that these segments are effective and can easily address any shortcomings if they are not. Since there is continual progress across the project lifecycle, this is thought to help reduce the risk of large-scale errors.

## How does APM work?

In their iterations, agile teams include quick feedback, constant adaptation, and QA best practices.

They use technologies to simplify measures to speed up the release and use of products, such as continuous distribution (CD) and continuous integration (CI).

Furthermore, Agile Project Management needs teams to measure time and expense as they go through their work. Instead of using Gantt charts and project goals to map success, they use velocity, burndown, and burnup charts to assess their work.

A project manager is not required to be present or participate in Agile Project Management. Although a project manager is essential for progress in conventional project-delivery methodologies like the Waterfall model (where the position oversees the budget, resources, project scope, efficiency, specifications, and other main elements), the project manager's function in APM is divided among team members.

The product owner, for example, sets project priorities, while team members divide up preparation, progress monitoring, and quality activities. Certain Agile approaches incorporate additional levels of management, such as the Scrum strategy, which requires a scrum master to help define goals and lead the project to completion.

Project developers, on the other hand, can also be found in Agile Project Management. Many companies do use project managers for Agile projects, particularly bigger, more complex ones, but these project managers are typically relegated to more of a planner position, with the product owner taking overarching responsibility for the project's completion.

Agile Project Management necessitates that team members understand how to function under this new environment, including the change in work from project managers to agile teams. They must be able to work together, both internally and with users. To keep tasks on schedule, they must be able to connect effectively. Therefore, they should be at ease taking the necessary steps at the appropriate times to meet distribution deadlines.

## APM's History

The Agile Project Management approach has become increasingly popular in the twenty-first century, especially for software development projects and other IT initiatives.

The idea of continuous growth, on the other hand, dates from the mid-twentieth century and has been advocated by numerous politicians over the decades in various ways. There was, for example, James Martin's Rapid Iterative Production Prototyping (RIPP), a method that served as the foundation for the 1991 book Rapid Application Development and the RAD approach.

Scrum is a particular Agile Project Management system that has developed in recent years. A project owner collaborates with a development team to build a design backlog, which is a prioritized list of functionality, functionalities, and updates needed to produce a viable software framework. The pieces are then delivered in quick succession by the squad.

**Waterfall vs. APM**

Agile Project Management was and continues to be a counter to cascade project management. The waterfall technique takes a step-by-step approach to projects, starting with collecting all specifications before beginning construction, scoping out the resources required, determining budgets and deadlines, doing the individual work, evaluating, and finally presenting the project as a whole until all work is done.

In 2001, 17 software developers released the Agile Manifesto, detailing 12 Agile Software Development concepts, in reaction to what they saw as flaws in the methodology. "Welcome evolving specifications, even late in the production," according to the principles, and "deliver working applications regularly."

Even now, Agile Project Management is driven by these concepts.

## Advantages and disadvantages

Agile project management proponents say that the technique has many advantages. This includes faster solution execution, more effective resource usage, greater flexibility and adaptability to evolving demands, faster problem discovery and faster repairs, and improved cooperation with customers, resulting in goods that best address customer needs.

However, certain disadvantages include a proclivity for proposals to deviate from their original course, a lack of reporting, and less consistent results.

Agile management is not appropriate for organizations that prefer to discuss problems for prolonged periods of time before taking action or delegating decision-making to a committee because it depends on the capacity to make swift decisions.

Agile project management is an iterative project management methodology that focuses on breaking down complex projects into smaller, more manageable activities that are performed in brief iterations over the course of the project life cycle. Agile teams are more able to finish work quicker, respond to evolving project needs, and streamline their processes.

Agile encourages teams to be more able to shift course and concentrate more easily, as the term implies. The propensity for project partners to shift from week to week is something that software companies and marketing firms are acutely aware of. The Agile approach encourages teams to re-evaluate their work and adapt in small steps so that the team's emphasis shifts as the task and consumer environment shift.

It can seem to be a complicated and difficult-to-manage scheme at first if you're new to agile project management. You're still doing all of the tasks Agile takes, whether you know it or not. You'll be on the way to faster production times and fewer, more regular product launches with a few tweaks.

**When it comes to project management, who uses Agile?**
The Agile project management methodology, which was first developed for software development, is rapidly being adopted by more than just IT teams. Marketers, universities, the military, and the car industry use Agile methodologies and systems to produce creative goods in uncertain environments. Agile project management can support a wide range of organizations, and it's easy to set up and use.

When deciding to create or improve an existing technology in the software environment, the final result can be difficult to describe. Agile allows for this uncertainty and it allows for project strategy to shift as construction progresses into the future.

Although Agile tools, books, and coaching can help you put together an Agile approach that works for you and your team, each Agile team is special, and learning the fundamentals can help you put together an Agile methodology that works for you and your team.

## What are the four fundamental Agile values?

The Agile Manifesto lays out four core values and twelve guiding principles that act as a compass for every team using the Agile approach.

## Agile's four core values are:

## 1. People and their experiences with systems and resources

No matter how advanced technology becomes, the human aspect will still play an important role in project management. When you depend so much on systems and resources, you won't be able to adjust to changing situations.

## 2. Working tech trumps thorough paperwork.

Working software is more critical than paperwork. This importance focuses on offering developers just what they need to complete their tasks without overburdening them.

## 3. Cooperation with customers rather than contract negotiations

One of your most valuable commodities is your clients. Involving consumers throughout the process, whether internal or external, will help to ensure that the final product serves their needs more efficiently.

## 4. Adapting to transition in accordance with a strategy

One of the most significant deviations from conventional project management is this importance. Shift has traditionally been seen as a cost to be minimized. Agile project management provides for ongoing progress over the duration of a project. Each sprint offers an opportunity to reflect on the previous sprint and make course corrections.

## What are the 12 agile principles?

The 12 Principles of Agile can still direct your choices and product creation. Agile methodologies should be as different and special as each particular team.

1. User satisfaction is our top priority, which we achieve by timely and consistent distribution of useful apps (or whatever else you deliver).

2. Be open to evolving conditions, even though they arrive late in the implementation process. Agile systems take advantage of transformation to help customers gain a strategic advantage.

3. Deliver tasks on a regular basis, anywhere from a few weeks to a few months, with a preference for the shorter timeframe.

4. During the project, members of the coordination committee would collaborate on a regular basis.

5. Assemble teams around people who are enthusiastic for their work. Provide them with the resources and resources they need and encourage them to complete the task.

6. The most reliable and productive way of conveying knowledge to and within various departments is face-to-face communication.

7. The finished result is the most important indicator of success.

8. Agile methods encourage long-term development. Both those involved should be able to keep up a steady tempo forever.

9. Maintaining a constant focus on technological performance and good architecture improves agility.

10. Simplicity is crucial—the art of minimizing the amount of work that isn't finished.

11. Self-organizing teams provide the right architectures, requirements, and prototypes.

12. The team focuses on ways to become more successful at frequent intervals, and tunes and changes the actions accordingly.

Agile project management's most important elements

**User testimonies**

Simply put, a user storey is a high-level description of a task. It provides only enough detail for the team to come up with a fair estimation of the time it would take to complete the submission. This brief, straightforward summary is written from the user's point of view and focuses on describing what the client needs (their objectives) and why.

**Sprints are a form of exercise that involves running**

Sprints are brief iterations that last one to three weeks and include teams working on projects that are decided at the sprint preparation meeting. As time goes by, the aim is to keep repeating these sprints until the app is feature-ready. During the sprint, you evaluate the product, see what is and isn't working, make changes, and start a new sprint to enhance the product or service.

**Meetings held in a standing position**

Regular stand-up sessions, also known as "daily Scrum meetings," are an excellent way to keep everyone on board and updated. The members are expected to remain standing during these regular encounters, which helps keep the meetings brief and point.

## A flexible board

An Agile board allows the team to keep track of your project's success. This can be a plain Kanban board, a whiteboard with sticky notes, or a feature of the project management program.

## A backlog of work

Plan requests become outstanding stories in the queue as they are added into the intake system. Your team will estimate storey points for each mission at agile preparation sessions. Stories from the backlog are pushed into the sprint to be finished of the iteration during sprint preparation. In an Agile environment, managing the backlog is critical for project managers.

## Roles in an agile squad

Depending on the Agile methodology, unique team tasks will be required to conform to the structure, or no roles may be required at all. While not every Agile implementation would necessitate any of these positions, here are a few that you may encounter:

• Scrum Master (Scrum Master). The Scrum Master keeps each sprint on target and assists in removing or resolving any problems or obstacles that may arise. They are the team's spokesman.

• The owner of the product. The product owner's job is to determine each sprint's priorities, handle and organize the team backlog, and act as the customer's or internal stakeholder's voice.

• Members of the team. This team's members are the ones who carry out the practice in each sprint. These teams, which often consist of three to seven people, can be made up of people with varying specialties and strengths or can be made up of people who have the same job positions.

• Stakeholders are people who have an interest in something. This is purely an informative role. Stakeholders should be kept informed about the product and sprint targets, given the opportunity to evaluate and support work during the sprint, and given the opportunity to provide input during the sprint retrospective.

Although . Agile technique has its own set of team members and tasks, there are a few common function characteristics that should be present in most Agile team structures:

1. T-shaped: A valuable Agile team member possesses a broad range of fundamental information about their subject, as well as in-depth knowledge, experience, and skill in one (or more) particular fields.

2. Cross-functionality: Cross-functionality is a term that refers to the ability to work through Agile team managers have abilities that go beyond their conventional roles. They may have a limited understanding of graphic design concepts and data processing and HTML/CSS.

3. Adaptable: If they have a wide range of skills, they know how to put them to good use. Their production is constant regardless of the climate.

4. Curious: Asking the right questions and changing the status quo where it's necessary is an important part of optimizing and being more effective.

5. Entrepreneurial: An Agile team manager is someone who does not wait for orders. Wherever they see a need, they're happy to step in and build campaigns.

6. Squad-oriented: Team leaders place a higher value on the team's performance than on their own personal fame. They consider it a success if everyone delivers on time and works well together.

7. Committed to excellence: One of the many advantages of Agile programs is the ability to achieve high-quality work more quickly. Team participants who are dedicated to perfection do not accept second best. They aren't perfectionists, but they are committed to doing their best work at all times.

## What are the agile methodology's six steps?

In comparison to conventional waterfall project management, Agile aims to deliver faster growth times and more regular product launches. Because of the shortened time span, project teams are more able to respond to shifts in the client's needs.

As previously said, you can use a variety of Agile systems, with Scrum and Kanban being two of the most common. However, each Agile approach will follow the same basic procedure, which involves the following steps:

## 1. Establishing a project schedule

Before starting any project, the staff should clearly understand the ultimate purpose, the importance to the company or customer, and how it can be accomplished.

You may create a project scope here, but keep in mind that the goal of agile project management is to be able to respond quickly to updates and improvements to the project, so the scope shouldn't be considered fixed.

## 2. Creation of a product roadmap

A roadmap is a list of items that will be used in the finished product. Since the team can create these individual features during each sprint, this is an important part of the Agile preparation stage.

You'll also create a project backlog at this stage, which is a list of all the features and deliverables that will go into the finished product. Your squad will take tasks from this backlog while planning sprints later.

## 3. Preparing for the release

In standard waterfall project management, a single execution deadline follows the completion of the whole project. When you use Agile, the project would have faster growth times (known as sprints), with features launched at the end of each iteration.

You'll create a high-level schedule for product updates before starting the project, and then you'll review and reassess the release plan for that feature at the start of each sprint.

## 4. Planning for a sprint

Before each sprint starts, the stakeholders must hold a sprint preparation meeting to decide what each individual will do during the sprint, how it will be done, and to assess the work load. It's critical to equally distribute the workload among team members so that they can complete their allocated tasks during the sprint.

For staff accountability, mutual knowledge, and finding and eliminating bottlenecks, you'll also need to chart the workflow visually.

## 5. Stand-ups every day

Hold short regular stand-up meetings to help the team complete their activities during each sprint and decide if any improvements are needed. Each team member will quickly discuss what they did the day before and what they will be focusing on the next day at these sessions.

These regular meetings can last no more than 15 minutes. They aren't intended to be lengthy problem-solving sessions or opportunities to discuss current events. To keep the conference short, certain departments will hold it standing up.

## 6. Retrospective and analysis of the sprint

Your team will have two meetings after each sprint ends: the first will be a sprint summary for project partners to present them the completed product. This is a crucial aspect of maintaining open lines of contact with stakeholders. All parties may create a partnership and address any product problems that occur during an in-person or video conference meeting.

Second, you'll have a sprint retrospective meeting with the partners to discuss what went well during the sprint, what should have gone well, if the work load was too high or too light for each team member, and what was achieved.

Don't miss this crucial meeting if the team is new to Agile project management. It allows you to determine how much the team will accomplish in and sprint as well as the most effective sprint duration for potential ventures.

**Making the switch to agile project management**
When you're about to go ahead with Agile, educate the Agile staff about how they'll adapt into their new positions, whether they'll start holding regular stand-up sessions, and how they'll transition their existing job into the Agile methodology.

You'll want to watch and chart their progress and results after you've established transformation measures and made sure everyone is happy with the new way of working.

What may be making them to struggle to run at the same speed as they did before? Are those statuses explicitly been established if the team isn't updating stories with their current status?

Tracking the development or performance of a new Agile team can be very helpful in instilling hope in the improvements. Furthermore, providing these Agile benchmarks will justify the gains of converting a team to Agile in higher-level sessions.

Finally, include a form to the staff and new Scrum Masters that addresses useful questions to pose at regular stand-ups and iteration retrospectives. This serves as outstanding evidence for subsequent procedure analyses. It will also enable the team to identify areas for improvement and answer questions that it may not have considered if it is new to Agile.

**Begin your Agile project management journey today.**

These are the most fundamental and critical components of Agile project management. These processes, Agile software and tools, roles, and principles will help you change your mindset and begin working together to be more flexible and adapt to changes as they come as you transition your team to an Agile methodology. Agile isn't for everyone, but it has a lot of advantages for teams who use it correctly, such as streamlined work processes and rapid innovation.

## What Is Agile Project Management Methodology?

The Agile methodology is a method of project management that divides a project into phases. It necessitates ongoing collaboration with stakeholders as well as continual improvement at each stage. Team's cycle through a process of planning, executing, and evaluating once the work begins. Collaboration is essential among team members as well as project stakeholders.

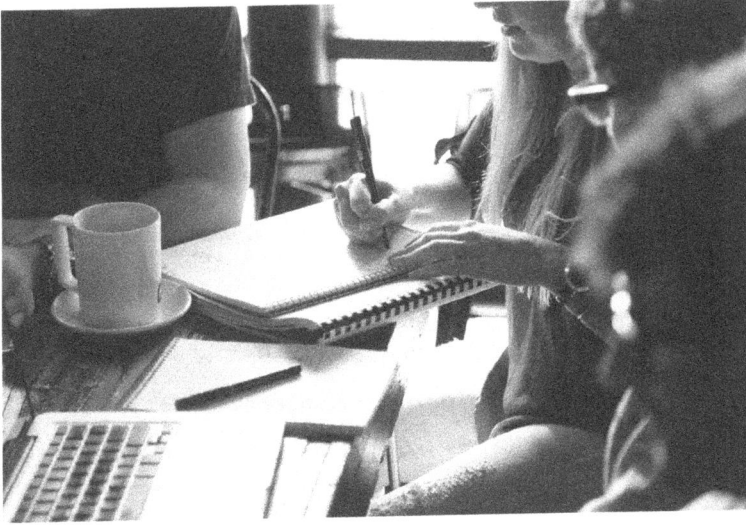

## Overview of Agile Methodologies

When it was first published in 2001, the Agile Manifesto of Software Development outlined a revolutionary approach to delivering value and collaborating with customers. The four main values of Agile are:

• People and their interactions with processes and tools

• Working software trumps thorough documentation.

• Collaboration with customers during contract negotiations

• Adapting to change in a planned manner

Frameworks for agile methodologies

So, what is agile project management methodology? It's a project management method that entails constant collaboration and iterative development. Scrum, Kanban, Extreme Programming (XP), and Adaptive Project Framework are examples of Agile frameworks that can be used to implement these values.

**Additional Reading:**

• Is It Time for Your Company to Become Agile? (Illustration)

• 8 Attitudes That Will Ensure Your Agile Projects Fail

• Is Agile a Good Option for Marketing Teams?

A project management method in which teams use sticky notes on whiteboards to create physical representations of their tasks. To track progress and identify common roadblocks, tasks are moved through predetermined stages.

## Scrum is a group of people who work together

Scrum is a project management methodology in which a small team is led by a Scrum master, whose primary responsibility is to remove all obstacles to completing work. The team meets daily to discuss current tasks and roadblocks. Work is done in short cycles called sprints.

## Framework for Adaptive Projects

The idea that most IT projects can't be managed using traditional PM methods spawned this project management methodology. Work is completed in stages, with each one being evaluated.

## The following are the four values of agile project management:

### 1. Individuals and Interactions vs. Tools and Processes

The Agile Manifesto's first value is "individuals and interactions over processes and tools." It basically means that people are valued more than processes or tools because people are the ones who respond to business/customer needs and move the process forward.

Tip: Ensure that communication is fluid and occurs only when it is required.

## 2. Working Software vs. Thorough Documentation

The Agile manifesto emphasises documentation, but working software is even more important. The Agile methodology focuses on streamlining data (software specifications, technical requirements, project prospectus, interface design papers, development plans, and so on) so that the developer can get down to business without being bogged down in the particulars.

Consider using an automated file management system instead of manual documentation.

## 3. Collaboration with customers takes precedence over contract negotiations.

Negotiation occurs right before the project delivery, when the customer and the manager/teams work out the details. On the other hand, the customer is not only engaged at the time of final delivery in the Agile Manifesto. Instead, during the development process, the

Agile approach engaged and collaborated with the customer.

Tip: At regular intervals, engage and collaborate with the customer for periodic demos. Assist your customer in becoming an integral part of the daily process, ensuring that you are meeting their needs.

## 4. Following a Plan in the Face of Change

Change was traditionally viewed as an extra cost, so it was avoided. On the other hand, change is viewed as a potential opportunity to improve and develop better results in the Agile manifesto.

Tip: At regular intervals, review your schedules, goals, and dependencies. Consider using Gantt chart or automated project planning software.

## What Are the Principles of Agile Project Management?

The following are the twelve Agile development principles:

• Early and continuous software delivery ensures customer satisfaction.

• Accept changes in requirements as part of the project management process.

• Use software sprints and iterations to deliver frequently.

• Collaborating throughout the project by ensuring continuous collaboration between business stakeholders, managers, and team members.

• Motivate teams so that they are more likely than unhappy teams to deliver their best work.

• Face-to-face interactions, especially when teams are co-located, to improve communication.

• To the customer, working software is a primary indicator of progress.

• Maintain a consistent rate of development.

• Excellent design and attention to detail to improve agility and ensure that teams continue improving the product and adapting to change.

• The ease with which you can develop just enough to get the job done right now (but without compromising the quality).

• Self-organization encourages teams to take ownership, communicate regularly, and deliver high-quality products by giving them decision-making power.

• Take time to reflect and adapt in order to improve your effectiveness and efficiency as a team.

What Is Agile Project Management and How Does It Work?

**Agile project management is a fascinating phenomenon that takes place in five stages:**

### Phase 1: Visualize

The imagine process is where the project's vision is created. It addresses the What, How, Where, and How of completing the project. The emphasis of this process is on the finished product and the project's scale.

### Phase 2: Conjecture

Speculation is the next step. This stage promotes brainstorming, teamwork, and innovative thinking on how the project can go forward. This is where everyone participating with the project talks about what's realistic and what's not, but still allowing for enough versatility to CHANGE if necessary.

## Phase 3: Investigate

The explore process is solely concerned with the delivery of project functionality.

Three key phrases are included in this phase:

• Managing the workload and adhering to best engineering practices and risk management techniques to ensure that the project is completed on time.

• Facilitated by the project manager, creating a self-organizing and inclusive society that bears responsibilities.

• Managing how members of the team communicate with one another and with outside parties (customers, product managers, stakeholders, etc).

## 4th Phase: Adapt

Modifications, updates, and fixes are made during the adapt process of the project management lifecycle. This step aims to compare the real findings to the expected ones. More specifically, thinking about the changes that need to be made and re-planning the strategy for the next version.

**Phase 5: Finish**

Now it's time for the final process. All involved with the project decides the project's endpoint even during this process. However, before they finish the job, they assess and evaluate all of the important things to ensure that they precisely achieve what is required.

**What's the Difference Between Traditional Project Management and Agile Project Management?**

There is little or no room for improvement in traditional project management. Only a rigid top-down approach is followed. When a proposal is made, everyone follows it as closely as possible.

Agile project design is more adaptable and has a lot of versatility when it comes to making improvements. People have the freedom to collaborate and play with the right ways to accomplish tasks.

## Transparency and ownership

Traditional project management: The Project Manager is solely responsible for the project's success. All is the duty of the manager to prepare, execute, and oversee. Simply put, the project managers have complete control of the project, and team members usually have no input in any part of it.

Managers, staff managers, and clients all have the same degree of project ownership in agile project management. All brings their heads together to prepare and complete the project in the time and budget allotted.

## Resolving issues

Traditional project management: If a problem or challenge arises, team members must contact the project manager for assistance. This triggers unnecessary complications which raises the total rate.

Agile project management: In the event of a problem, teams have the authority to make decisions on their own. They are capable of resolving all conflicts individually, eliminating the waste of time. Crew members may, however, recommend escalating to their boss if they need to make drastic decisions.

## Checkpoints and success reporting

Traditional project management: Extensive preparation is needed during the project's research and design stages. The emphasis is entirely on streamlining operations rather than the commodity itself. With limited feedback and no regular check-ins, the team follows a step-by-step, predefined plan.

Team participants are encouraged to provide checkpoints at frequent intervals as part of agile project management. They have regular stand-ups to share information about what progress has been completed, what challenges have been encountered, how they have been addressed, and what work needs to be completed tomorrow.

## The agile principles

Today, agile project management is already driven by 12 main concepts.

1. Customer loyalty is still first and foremost, and it is accomplished by timely and consistent execution.

2. Changing environments are welcomed at every point of the process in order to offer a comparative edge to the consumer.

3. A good or service is offered on a more regular basis.

4. On a regular basis, stakeholders and entrepreneurs work closely together.

5. All partners and team members are kept engaged for the best possible project results, and teams are given the appropriate resources and encouragement and are trusted to meet project objectives.

6. The most reliable and effective format for project progress is face-to-face meetings.

7. The ultimate criterion for quality is the finished working product.

8. Sustainable development is achieved by agile processes that enable development teams and partners to work consistently and continuously.

9. Agility is improved by maintaining a constant emphasis on technological competence and careful design.

10. Simplicity is a key component.

11. Self-organizing teams are most likely to come up with the right architectures and designs, as well as reach deadlines.

12. Teams use regular intervals to fine-tune habits and increase performance.


The tech industry created agile to help streamline and optimize the production process so that issues and errors could be identified and corrected quickly. It allows developers and teams to produce a stronger product in a shorter amount of time by using quick, immersive iterative sessions/sprints. Agile is a natural match for organizations trying to reinvent how they handle programs and function as a whole in the era of digital change, with many firms migrating to a modern workspace. Agile will assist with ensuring methodology and methodological consistency across the organization. Both the digital workspace and agile have the following market benefits: • Increased versatility • Increased efficiency

• Improvements in accountability

• Deliverables of higher quality

• There's a lower chance of missing a goal.

• Increased stakeholder loyalty and participation

The benefits of agile project management

Agile project design offers numerous project-specific advantages to project teams, supporters, project participants, and clients, including:

• Technologies can be deployed more quickly.

• Services were used more efficiently, resulting in less pollution.

• Increased adaptability and versatility in the face of transition

• Greater progress as a result of more concentrated activities

• Reduced processing time

- Faults and flaws are detected more quickly.

- Methods for production that are more efficient

- A structure that is less heavy

- Optimal project management

- A greater emphasis on particular consumer requirements

- Increased communication and feedback level

**The disadvantages of agile**

Like every other technique, Agile isn't right for every project, and it's definitely a good idea to do your homework and figure out which approach works better for your specific case. If a customer's goals are unclear, the project manager or team is inexperienced, or they do not perform well under pressure, Agile cannot operate as expected. Agile favors engineers, project teams, and client goals during the creation process, but not generally the end user's experience. Agile cannot often be readily absorbed within bigger, more hierarchical organizations with considerable levels of rigidity or flexibility within systems, procedures, or departments due to the less organized and more fluid processes. It can also encounter issues as used by consumers that have identical static systems or operating procedures.

# Chapter 2 How to Apply Agile Project Management

Agile will greatly improve the odds of a project's completion if it's integrated into the way it's managed. Many organizations, however, struggle to implement agile project management due to a lack of experience, leadership, and expertise.

Since there isn't a 100% guarantee that the process will go smoothly, certain aspects of the industry and society must be examined and planned to be successful for the Agile implementation.

Let's start with the major organizational barriers to Agile adoption. Following that, we'll go through seven key concepts to consider and improve in order to add true agility to your business.

## Obstacles to Agile Adoption in the Workplace

In our experience, many companies face a variety of traditional roadblocks while attempting to implement agile project management.

**The business ethos or structure does not well support the Agile theory:**

This is a typical situation. A new project manager with Agile vision, for example, joins a team and explains the advantages of Agile project management and development. And if the project management embraces the concept and seems to be keen for transition, the remainder of the organization may not be. For Agile to be fully sustainable, executives and leaders must embrace the vision and support the Agile philosophy.

The corporation is unaware of the consequences for its corporate priorities and overall vision:

Following the Agile mindset while managing tasks would not be enough to achieve the necessary gains from the agile implementation. Assume that the organization's strategic alignment isn't present at all stages. In that case, ventures can also be handled in ways that do not produce the optimal outcomes for your whole enterprise, preventing you from achieving long-term success.

**Agile skills are lacking or limited:**

Regardless of how successful Agile is, finding and attracting top agile talent can be difficult. And this stumbling block reduces the opportunities of agile project management for businesses.

**Top Agile talent should have the following essential skills:**

1. The opportunity to concentrate on the most important tasks while avoiding the ones that aren't.

2. The ability to stay confident in the face of adversity and make good decisions

3. Strong inspiration and organizational skills to support and direct the team through the process.

4. The ability to think quickly and make swift choices in a fast-changing environment

5. High adaptability, especially in rapidly changing environments or circumstances

6 Aspects to Examine and Improve for a Successful Agile Launch

Concentrate on Flow Performance, rather than Capacity Utilization.

Rather than maximizing power usage, effective Agile project execution necessitates an emphasis on optimizing movement. A popular belief in conventional project management is that the operation would be successful if all tools are properly used. In fact, however, this is simply incorrect.

Since everyone is busy doing their own thing, full capacity usage also causes a non-collaborative atmosphere where information exchange is rare. People are often overburdened and treated as "robots," resulting in poor efficiency.

That is why we follow the Agile mantra of "manage the job, not the workers" in our programs. The emphasis is on improving flow performance, which is described as the ratio of value-adding time to total lead time in a process. Agile teams strive to continually minimize waste in order to bring value to the market more efficiently.

The easiest way to do this in practice is to imagine all of your process's value-adding and non-value-adding operations. The use of a Kanban board, where teams map their operation from beginning to end, is a common practice. This helps them see what's going on at a glance and where they need to take steps (like removing bottlenecks) to improve work flow.

Engaging in a method known as "swarming" is one of the easiest ways to improve the flow performance of the process. This ensures that after a staff member completes a mission, instead of simply moving on to new jobs, they go around the board and assist their peers. Swarming fosters organizational collaboration which works on improving the collective process rather than individual changes.

Not timelines, however queue sizes can be managed.

Orthodox project management places a strong emphasis on developing comprehensive schedules and keeping track of deadlines. That, though, does not fit in a knowledge-based workplace where change is constant.

As a result, a good agile implementation needs project managers to shift their emphasis from deadlines to queue size management. Of course, there must always be a strategy in motion. However, this occurs in the project and is only a matter of time. To put it another way, we don't build overly prescriptive schedules in Agile that force our team members to finish their assignments on time.

Instead, project managers in an Agile environment can minimize turnaround time and improve the performance of the project management process by focusing on queues. This gives them more leverage over project schedules and helps them to complete projects faster.

You must imagine the queues to ensure that they do not get too long. This can happen on a Kanban monitor, where you can see where activities are piling up at a glance and easily investigate why.

**Reduce the number of work items in each batch.**

Reducing batch sizes is an important part of completing any project successfully in a knowledge-based world. Small batches of work will run more smoothly through the project's workflow, resulting in longer feedback loops and less variability.

You will lower the average cost of your project by reducing the batch size of your work pieces. Per method has a different optimum job batch size. Consider the tiniest possible bit of work that can collect merit and come up with that.

You will be able to deal with new changes and challenges more easily after you have done so. As a result, instead of major reworks, you'll make only minor changes where possible, saving project money and increasing the chances of pleasing the end user.

**Work In Progress (WIP) Constraints should be implemented.**

To effectively incorporate Agile in project management, you must handle queues efficiently, as we previously said. Using WIP restrictions is one of the most effective ways to do this. The term "work in progress" refers to the number of projects that a team actively works on. Having too many open work items triggers regular background switches, raises the chance of rework, and wastes time in the operation.

To address this problem, you must first apply WIP limits for your different work phases, and then re-adjust them as required. When a given step of the workflow hits its cap, no additional items can be included. Limiting work in progress (WIP) will help you match your team's ability to the total amount of tasks that need to be accomplished at any given time. This leads to a rise in Flow, a decrease in multitasking, and, as a result, a boost in the team's productivity.

With the assistance of the Kanban board, it is possible to apply WIP limits in operation. You will restrict the number of tasks in each column there. This establishes rules for the team members to move assignments from one level to the next, avoiding bottlenecks and long lines.

**Fast Feedback Loops Should Be Incorporated**
Quick feedback loops must be integrated into every Agile project execution.

Short feedback loops are critical for Agile project management progress because they enable teams to learn quickly and make appropriate project changes.

When introducing Agile in your company, make sure you have a mechanism in place so you can regularly sync your work outcomes with your customers and get feedback. This would enable you to change your product or service growth strategy in a timely manner, allowing you to fulfill your customers' needs properly.

**Decentralized decision-making is a good idea.**

To achieve value in the shortest and most sustainable timeframe, an effective Agile deployment necessitates decentralized power.

Any decision in conventional project management must go through many "high-authority" approval processes before it can be implemented. This causes significant project delays and lowers the team's morale.

On the other hand, decentralized decision-making provides more leverage to the departments who are nearest to the technical aspects of the job. Of course, this does not imply that "everyone is free to do whatever they want." Instead, it entails collaborating with team mates, respectfully listening to their opinions, and encouraging them to make decisions on how to carry out their responsibilities better.

This idea improves the efficiency of the process and gives the team members a feeling of belonging. As a result, they'll be more likely to contribute to the project's ultimate progress because they'll see themselves as important assets rather than disposable tools.

## 6 Points to Consider for a Smooth Agile Project Management Transition

### 1) Determine the company's objectives.

Until implementing a new project management approach, it's critical to define and frame your business objectives and explain how switching to Agile project management will help you achieve them. There must be a good understanding of how the current approach can help project teams meet the company's objectives.

## 2) Examine whether the company's culture is "fit for function."

One of the most important prerequisites for embarking on the Agile development journey is to have the right soil, i.e., a culture that is not afraid of transition. This involves getting top leadership and expertise and meeting the seven basic criteria for learning Agile skills. They must be able to conform to Agile standards and help them. Transparency and regular contact will help to make this process go more smoothly.

## 3) Examine the possible consequences for your clients.

It's critical to figure out how Agile can impact your customers and how this transition will help the team to fulfill their expectations and needs. Here are three questions to ask yourself to help you figure out what effect you could have on your customers:

• How can implementing Agile boost the consumer experience?

• Would this transition result in improved deliverables and a higher level of quality?

• Can Agile assist the company in properly collaborating with its clients and teams?

## 4) Examine all of the company's available capital.

Attempt to recognize all of the company's project capital. Is your organization equipped with the necessary talent and skill sets to implement Agile to its full potential? Will you have the right resources in place to support emerging technologies and suppliers that will help you make the transition to Agile smoothly? It is critical to get the best personnel and technologies in order to reap the Agile benefits.

## 5) Enlist the assistance of the company's executives right away.

The transition to a modern project management methodology is a significant step with implications for systems, staff, and technologies. Engage the company's executives and consultants right away to help you figure out the best way to work with the inevitable changes while keeping the Agile project management plan intact.

## 6) Before the major roll-out, start with a few minor tasks.

If you're introducing Agile in your business, don't make any drastic changes to large ventures right away. Instead, if at all necessary, carry out the latest method on a few small projects or various sections of a larger project.

This will help you to determine the level of resistance within your team and test the climate. As a result, you'll be able to make appropriate changes and work with your colleagues to adapt the recently introduced agile approach to your specific needs.

### How Will Agile Be Used in the Testing Process?

**The following are crucial moves in applying the agile methodology:**

### At the initial strategy meeting, define your vision.

Before you start an agile project, you need to figure out who your target buyer is, what your client's market is about, what the product's branding and category is, what its core features and advantages are, and how it differs competitors.

And if the project's end aim isn't to create a product, you can also change the targets to suit the project's objectives. This meeting clarifies the project's core features, so key stakeholders such as product owners, administrators, administrators, and executives can attend. You can divide the meeting into various time spans, so you can plan on spending 4 to 16 hours to get the point through.

## Developing a Product Roadmap

The project owner would then convert the vision outlined in the meeting into a product plan after the approach has been confirmed. The product roadmap is a high-level overview of the specifications that is accompanied by a timeline forecast.

We don't schedule every detail of the project in this step; instead, we classify, prioritize, and predict how much effort and time each part would need. The most effective approach to build an effective roadmap is to include quick goals in the overall strategy.

Each of these milestones should include five main pieces of information: name, date, target, features, and metrics. Despite the fact that the Product Owner develops the blueprint, he or she must consult key stakeholders and members from production, testing, promotion, distribution, and help.

It's important to note that these roadmap meetings should be held immediately after your strategy meeting and before you begin preparing sprints.

**Carry on with the Release Plan.**

It's time to build established deadlines once you've developed a strategy and a schedule. The product owner creates a high-level timeline for the testing phase at this stage. Due to the fact that agile programs have multiple launches, product owners must select the functionality that they need right away. The duration of your sprints and the size of your tasks will determine this. A release schedule usually takes 3–5 sprints to complete.

Everyone on the working committee is included with the release process. As a result, everybody is expected to attend this conference, including the product owner, project managers, and team members.

**Sprint Planning**

The release schedule, of course, contributes to sprint preparation. The product owner and the testing team meet here to determine which projects and priorities can be completed first.

These sprint training sessions result in a backlog of things to work on. At the start of each sprint period, this meeting must take place. If you're doing weekly sprints, for example, it's important to have a planning session every Monday (or any other day you decided).

## Have the Team on Track with Regular Stand-Ups

A regular stand-up is a fifteen-minute meeting that must be held to ensure that the proposal does not encounter any roadblocks. It aids in the tracking of your team's progress by keeping track of the work completed each day and scheduling new assignments for the day.

While some team members dislike these sessions, they must maintain a clear line of contact between various teams and their superiors. It also meets the demands of agile project management, which necessitates fast problem resolution and improved cross-team coordination.

Sprint Cycle Completion and Sprint Review

You must assess success and determine what the team has accomplished in terms of the objectives set out. To begin, make sure that all of the criteria have been met.

Accepting or rejecting functionalities completed during this period is up to the product managers. If something goes wrong, the product owner must understand why. Around the same time, they must change the next sprint in order for their team to meet the next set of goals. It's normal to have a few hiccups at the beginning because Agile relies on continuous learning and iterations.

The sprint summary meeting can last no more than an hour or two. All main stakeholders and the whole staff must be present at the meeting so that you can check progress transparently and enable all participants to express their concerns.

## The Cycle Goes On

Agile project management is based on a step-by-step approach that is aided by a coordination and accountability process. After a single sprint is done, take a look at which features have been completed and what the team has to do next.

The product owner would understand what needs to be changed in the project's original schedule and vision. You will use the lessons learned from a finished sprint to develop a strategy that is suitable for the whole team. Since this retrospective is a follow-up to the analysis, you'll need input from the rest of the team.

It's impossible to plan new additions or fixes before you get input on finished work. The reviews and increments loop must continue until the project is over.

Rather than digging into the backlog, the staff can look at client reviews and see how consumers respond to it.

**Agile vs. Scrum: What's the Difference?**

Agile and Scrum seem to be somewhat similar on the surface, as both depend on an iterative approach, regular customer engagement, and collective decision-making. The primary distinction between Agile and Scrum is that, while Agile is a project management framework based on a core collection of standards or concepts, Scrum is a specialized Agile approach for project management.

Other noticeable distinctions between Agile and Scrum can also be seen.

Differences include:

• Scrum is a kind of Agile approach, while Agile is a theory.

• Scrum is divided into smaller sprints and deliverables, while Agile delivers all at the end of the project.

• Agile projects have participants from a variety of cross-functional organizations, while Scrum project teams include specialized positions such as the Scrum Master and Product Owner.

It's important to note that, while Scrum is an Agile approach, Agile does not necessarily imply Scrum—there are a variety of Agile project management methodologies.

### Other Methodologies vs. Agile

Although Agile and Scrum get a lot of press, a few other methodologies are to be informed of. Here's how Agile stacks up against Waterfall and Kanban, two common project management methodologies.

## Waterfall vs. Agile

Waterfall project management is another common method for project management that differs from Agile. Waterfall is sequential in nature and does not allow for revisiting prior steps and processes, whereas Agile is an iterative and flexible approach to project management.

Waterfall is suitable for small projects with simple end targets, while Agile is better for large projects with more complexity. Another significant distinction between these two methods is the degree of stakeholder participation. Clients are seldom present in Waterfall projects, although customer feedback is critical in Agile.

## Kanban vs. Agile

Kanban project management is an Agile methodology that aims to improve project management by visualizing workflows using a tool called a Kanban board. A Kanban board comprises columns representing different stages in the project management process, with cards or sticky notes representing tasks assigned to each stage. The cards will switch from column to column on the board as the project continues before it is done.

One of the main differences between Kanban and other Agile methodologies, such as Scrum, is that there are usually limits on the number of tasks that can be completed at any given time. In most cases, project management teams will attribute a specific number of tasks to each column on the board, which means that new tasks cannot begin until the previous ones are completed.

**Choosing the Right Project Methodology: Agile vs. Scrum**

You can start thinking about applying Agile and Scrum to your own projects once you understand what they are and how they work together. However, given the differences between the two, it shouldn't be a question of choosing between Agile and Scrum.

Instead, if you determine that an Agile approach is the best fit for your project, the next question is which Agile methodology to use. Scrum or one of the several other Agile methodologies may be the solution.

You'll need to look at the specific constraints and requirements involved in your project to see if Agile is right for it. Agile was born in the sense of software development programs and has proven to be especially successful in this field. With this in mind, Agile would not work on projects with very strict scope and implementation specifications. The Agile philosophy's driving principles, on the other hand, are commonly used in a diverse range of project forms.

If you evaluate that an Agile approach is right for your project, you'll need to figure out whether Scrum is the best Agile methodology for your needs and objectives. Scrum is best suited to projects with ambiguous requirements, a high likelihood of change, and/or frequent testing.

It's important to remind that the key to a successful project isn't just picking the right methodology; it's also executing it effectively. This necessitates a thorough understanding of the methodology you ultimately choose and other crucial project management skills. Project managers must also be able to communicate effectively, lead a team, apply problem-solving and critical thinking skills, and be adaptable to the organizational complexities and dynamics around them in order to be successful in their roles.

"This is why technical skills should be viewed as just one component of the skills required to lead projects successfully," Griffin says. "This is why Northeastern's project management program focuses on developing competencies in teamwork, communication, leadership, critical thinking, problem-solving, and organizational awareness, rather than just technical skills."

Griffin explains that students in Northeastern's Graduate Certificate in Agile Project Management program and the Agile concentration in the Master of Science in Project Management program learn about Agile methodologies. More importantly, students pursuing an advanced degree in project management learn how to execute projects in a skilled and mature manner from seasoned professionals who have spent years honing their own skills in the field.

What Is Agile Scrum Methodology and How Does It Work?

What are some of the advantages of the agile scrum methodology?

Here are a few of the many advantages of the agile scrum methodology:

• Adaptability and flexibility

• Ingenuity and creativity

- Cost-cutting

- Enhancement of quality

- Organizational cohesion

- Employee contentment

- Customer contentment

The most significant advantage of the agile scrum methodology is its adaptability. The scrum team typically gets feedback from stakeholders after each sprint in the sprint-based model. If any issues or changes arise, the scrum team can easily and quickly adjust product goals in future sprints, resulting in more valuable iterations. Stakeholders are happier in this scenario because they get exactly what they want after being involved at every stage.

In traditional project management systems, stakeholders do not provide frequent feedback, and time is wasted making changes to the product halfway through development – or, worse, the teams must start over after the product has been built.

To implement agile scrum methodology, either an internal scrum expert or an external scrum consultant must be present to ensure that scrum principles are applied correctly. Agile scrum methodology necessitates precise execution, which if not done correctly, can lead to disaster.

## What do the various roles in the agile scrum methodology entail?

There are two types of roles in the Agile scrum methodology: core roles (also known as "pigs") and ancillary roles (also known as "chickens").

Scrum master, product owner, and scrum team are the three main roles. These individuals are all dedicated to the scrum project.

Scrum master, for starters. The scrum master is the scrum development process's facilitator. The scrum master ensures that scrum rules are enforced and applied as intended, in addition to holding daily meetings with the scrum team. Coaching and motivating the team, removing sprint impediments, and assuring that the team has the best possible conditions to meet its goals and produce deliverable products are all part of the scrum master's responsibilities.

2. Owner of the product. Stakeholders, which are typically customers, are represented by the product owner. The product owner determines product expectations, records product changes, and administers a scrum backlog, a constantly updated and detailed to-do list for the scrum project, to ensure the scrum team is always delivering value to stakeholders and the business. The product owner is also in charge of prioritizing sprint goals based on stakeholder value, ensuring that the most deliverable and important features are built in each iteration.

## 3. The Scrum team

It is a self-organized group of three to nine people with the business, design, analytical, and development skills needed to complete tasks, solve problems, and deliver products. Scrum team members self-administer tasks and are jointly responsible for achieving each sprint's objectives.

Other stakeholders who are involved in the scrum project but are not committed to it are referred to as ancillary roles. Members, customers and management, of the executive team are typically involved in ancillary roles for reporting progress, consulting, and gathering feedback to better work toward delivering the highest value possible.

What are the distinctions between scrum and agile development?

Despite the similarities between scrum and agile, there are a few key differences:

• Scrum emphasizes rigidity, while agile emphasizes flexibility.

• Agile leaders are critical, and scrum encourages a self-contained cross-functional team.

• Agile emphasizes face-to-face interactions with members of cross-functional teams, while scrum emphasizes regular stand-up meetings.

• Agile is intended to be basic, while scrum can be imaginative and creative.

## Chapter 3 Agile software production techniques

Scrum, Extreme Programming, and Feature-Driven Development are examples of agile software development environments (FDD).

Pair programming, test-driven development, stand-ups, strategy meetings, and sprints are all examples of agile software development techniques.

The Manifesto for Agile Software Development and its 12 Principles are an umbrella concept for a collection of systems and strategies focused on the ideals and principles expressed in the Manifesto for Agile Software

Development. When approaching software development in a certain way, it's basically a smart idea to abide by these values and concepts and use them to help you find out what to do in your own situation.

Agile differs from other software development methodologies in that it focuses on the people doing the work and how they collaborate. Collaboration of self-organizing cross-functional teams using the best practises for their context leads to solutions.

The Agile software development culture places a strong emphasis on teamwork and the self-organizing team.

That isn't to say there aren't any managers. It means that groups can work out how they're going to solve problems on their own.

Those departments are cross-functional, in other words. Those teams don't need to have unique roles; instead, they can make sure they have all of the necessary skill sets before they're put together.

Managers have a place in the world. Managers ensure that team members possess or acquire the necessary skill sets. Managers provide an atmosphere in which the team can succeed. Managers typically take a step back to let their teams work out how to produce goods, but they step in as the teams attempt but fail to fix problems.

When most teams and companies begin using Agile growth, they concentrate on activities that aid in teamwork and task management, which is awesome. Basic engineering approaches that closely deal with designing apps that let the team deal with complexity are another important group of practices that are not widely practiced but should be. Those technical procedures are critical and should not be overlooked.

### Agile's Brief History

Here's how Agile came to be, how it got the name Agile, and where it went from there. It's important to consider where Agile software development comes from in order to understand where things are now.

### Agile is a state of mind.

Finally, Agile is a mindset based on the ideals and beliefs of the Agile Manifesto. These ideals and principles show

how to build and adapt to transition, as well as how to cope with confusion.

The Agile Manifesto's first statement encapsulates the whole concept: "We are discovering new ways of creating apps by doing so and helping others do so."

When faced with ambiguity, try something you think could fit, get feedback, and make adjustments if needed.

When you're doing this, have the ideals and beliefs in mind. Allow the background to inform the frameworks, strategies, and procedures you use to communicate with your team and provide value to your customers.


## What are Agile Methodologies and How Do They Work?

What does it mean if Agile is a mindset? What does it mean if Agile methodologies are a mindset? It might be useful to provide a good understanding of technique to address this issue.

According to Alistair Cockburn, a technique is a collection of conventions that a group chooses to obey. That ensures that each team will have its own approach, which will vary from the methodologies of the other teams in small or significant ways.

As a result, Agile methodologies are the conventions that a team prefers to adopt when adhering to Agile values and concepts.

"Wait, I thought Scrum and XP were Agile methodologies," you're probably thinking. Alistair coined the word "system" to describe such ideas. They were definitely born from the methodology of a single person, but they were constructs until they were adapted for use by other teams. Those structures will help a team decide where to begin with their technique, but they should not be the approach itself. To suit better with its setting, the team would need to change the use of a system on a regular basis.

What about Agile Business Analysis or Agile Project Management?

When Agile Software Development became more common, people who were interested in software development but didn't design software looking for a way to understand how these Agile concepts related to their line of work.

A community of software developers (and a tester) wrote the Agile Manifesto and the 12 Principles to fix software developers' challenges. When you think about Agile as a mindset, you should apply it to a variety of tasks.

Agile becomes an adjective when you do this. It explains how you go about doing that. For the reasons mentioned above, it does not establish a new technique.

Ask yourself, "How can we practice project management in a way that helps us to build and adapt to change and cope with uncertainty?" if you want to consider Agile project management. The Agile Alliance and the Project Management Institute (PMI) collaborated on the Agile Practice Guide to answer this issue (Available to Agile Alliance Members).

Ask yourself, "How can we conduct market analysis in a way that helps us to build and adapt to change and cope with uncertainty?" if you want to consider Agile business analysis. The Agile Alliance and the International Institute of Business Analysis (IIBA) collaborated on the Agile Extension of the Business

Analysis Body of Knowledge to investigate this topic (Available to Agile Alliance Members).

## What about the definition of business agility?

The two ideas described above are attempts to take Agile "outside of tech." The Business Agility revolution has recently emerged as a result of these activities.

People pursuing Business Agility ask themselves, "How should we organize and run our organization in a way that helps us to build and respond to change and deal with uncertainty?" If Agile is viewed as a mentality, then people seeking Business Agility ask themselves, "How might we structure and operate our organization in a way that enables us to develop and react to change and deal with uncertainty?"

Company agility may be described as the understanding that in order for individuals in an organization to work with an agile mentality, the entire organization must endorse it. Agile software development was never fully agile until the organization's structure and operations were modified to accommodate working in an unstable world.

## Which of the Agile Software Development Methodologies Do You Use?

Methodologies for software creation are extremely important.

As a non-technical startup designer, you must be mindful of the various SDMs that could be employed during your construction process. The SDM you choose explains how the production team can respond to various situations in the project.

Will they, for example, waste a significant amount of time at the start designing a schedule that cannot be changed? (plan-focused). Will the development team priorities feature development and respond to roadblocks as needed? (feature-focused). By deciding on the production process style early on, the project starts with reasonable priorities, helping the startup to keep track of the project's success.

Choosing an SDM is an important phase in the implementation process. This is because the most significant risk of software development failure is the selection of an inappropriate technique. Choosing the wrong tactic will result in project budget overruns, schedule delays, and a lack of requirement verification, all of which are called project failures.

## Software Development Methodologies: Traditional vs. Agile

Takeaway: During development, the startup will use either conventional or agile approaches. Traditional preparation necessitates a considerable amount of forethought. Agile, on the other hand, helps you to respond to problems when they arise.

One of the first choices you'll have to make before beginning construction is which approach the startup can take. Will the company take a conventional (predictive) or agile (adaptive) approach? The majority of active startups take an agile approach, which industry experts also suggest.

A conventional solution necessitates extensive upfront preparation. The team conducts a rigorous requirement review and maps out the project from start to finish until starting construction. That can function very well in a predictable setting. It can backfire disastrously in a startup.

AOnthe other hand, ian agile strategy nvolves no comprehensive preparation and only the identification of straightforward possible tasks. The majority of the time, this approach is applicable to startups because agile software development methodologies allow for:

• Shifts in the software product's specifications that are dynamic.

• Consistent research, as well as

• Communications with the customer on a regular basis

Among these diverse divisions of conventional and agile techniques, there are several strategies. Let's take a closer look at each of the various approaches applicable to your startup now.

Expancio is a case study from the RIC Centre.

Expancio is a startup that offers a tool to assist companies in the planning, developing, and managing their web applications. Businesses do not need to construct a web application from the ground up for their product. Instead, they can use Expancio's network, which will save them a lot of money on growth.

When Expancio began receiving calls for service from companies and began signing contracts, the team realized they needed a strategy. This strategy had to include how the team would effectively and effectively complete each mission.

His choice was based on his previous experience developing web apps for financial institutions. The Waterfall Methodology is widely used in the finance sector, where the whole construction process must be meticulously prepared before any work can begin. Banks would then adhere to a rigid production schedule that made it difficult to respond to developments in the business or sector.

The development of a series of comprehensive conceptual plans enhanced the project's scope, which was Lee's biggest challenge when employed in the finance sector. This complication arose from attempting to schedule out an entire construction program, including all possible phases of development, before any planning had been done. The amount of money and time taken to complete the project increased as the project's complexity grew.

Instead, the banks should have used agile software development methodologies in their implementation phases. Lee should have developed the requisite software product in tiny stages using agile techniques, with in-development testing incorporated directly into the project schedule. Lee and the rest of the marketing team may have developed the requisite product using these agile approaches, rather than relying on upfront preparation, and instead letting the outcomes of in-development product tests guide the remaining development phases.

When it came to deciding the approach Expancio could use during product development, Lee proposed agile development methodologies based on all of his previous experiences. Expancio, as a startup, must be able to respond easily to trends in the market in order to ensure that their product and business do not fall behind.

Expancio will also continue to verify their early commercial offering using agile growth methodologies. Agile methodologies enable the organization to easily adjust their platform in response to customer input, allowing for constant validation. Any user observations about task fulfillment problems and implementation defects and vulnerabilities found within the product can be solved at a new iteration period. Expancio is able to build a product that their customers actually like by iterating their early stage commercial product during the validation process. Instead of saving all opportunities for customer input at the very end of production, where a major redesign of the product could be needed, this method is used.

Overall, Expancio's platform will continue to evolve and expand thanks to the use of agile implementation methodologies. This means that their offering does not get stale, and that it can easily be changed in response to customer reviews and market developments.

## Methodologies used in traditional app creation

The main takeaway is that traditional development methodologies are heavily hierarchical and allow for little versatility throughout the development process. The Waterfall Technique is the most popular conventional approach used by startups.

Traditional architecture methodologies produce designs with a lot of structure. They are built on a sequence of plan-driven moves that follow one another.

Until beginning production, the team maps out the whole process during the definition stage. This is done to assist participants during the project's work process.

Until beginning growth, many startups do not have explicitly validated product specifications. This can be a difficult task. As a consequence, money could be squandered on progress that may need to be updated as specifications change.

Software engineers widely use orthodox methodologies on projects that are:

• Large budgets (usually in excess of $1 million) that allow for the redoing of work

• Multiple medium-sized teams working on a similar initiative use it.

• Large corporations are in charge of the project.

Traditional approaches are now the most often used implementation model, despite the popularity of agile software development methodologies.

**Advantages include:**

• An easy-to-understand plan-driven method

• All staff members have strict production responsibilities.

• Capable of working in big groups and programs

Contrary to popular belief, there are a number of disadvantages of using this method.

• The cost of restarting the construction process is high.

• Startups must know the software specifications from the beginning of the project.

• A rigid production process with little or no room for error

• Testing is usually done at the conclusion of the production phase.

There are a variety of common methodologies, all of which are focused on the central principle of organizing the project ahead of time to drive growth. It's crucial to figure out which conventional approach is best for the project. If your startup chooses an approach that emphasizes organizing ahead of time, you must prepare appropriately.

The Waterfall model is the most applicable to startups. The following section outlines the core standard methodologies available, starting with the most relevant to startups, the Waterfall model.


**Model of a waterfall**

The Waterfall model is ideally fit for startups with projects that have well-defined, well-understood criteria that are unlikely to modify. Strict reporting and preparation limits construction flexibility when dealing with design issues.

The Waterfall model (also known as the linear-sequential life cycle model or cascade model) necessitates the completion and analysis of each growth stage before moving on to the next (Figure 2). This model necessitates substantial paperwork to ensure that the project sticks to the schedule and develops all of the requested specifications. This amount of reporting can be overwhelming for new businesses.

Loops can be used to enable the user to return to a previous level. This enables the startup to carry out product testing..

Advantages: • Thanks to the high quality of documentation and structural architecture, new team members can quickly join; • Coordination is simple since each stage has a planned outcome and assessment process.

• Consists of a series of steps that team members should follow and understand.

• Has a set of stages that must be completed in order.

• Due to a fixed timeline and services that are distributed appropriately, determining project costs becomes simple.

Contrary to popular belief, there are a number of disadvantages of using this method.

• At the outset of the process, all requirements must be thoroughly understood.

• Identifying additional standards has a negative effect on growth, rising costs and delaying the timetable.

• Restricts production flexibility, making it impossible to return to the design stage if experimentation reveals a flaw.

• Creates a prototype with customer input at the conclusion of the production period, rather than through it.

• Due to a lack of stability, the proposal is at a high risk.

For the following situations, it is suggested:

• Projects with well-defined, well-articulated, and final specifications

• A well-understood technology with a well-defined, repeatable implementation route (not innovative)

• Short assignments with a low risk of the customer requesting extra specifications

• Whether you have Subject Matter Experts (SMEs) on your staff who can map out the project before production starts.

• Software that offers back-end services or serves as a tool to other programs.

## Model for prototyping

The prototyping paradigm is ideally fit for startups working on projects with ambiguous specifications and a strong emphasis on the user experience. Significant customer participation almost often lengthens the project's time and costs.

Prototyping is the process of quickly creating a prototype of a finished product's capability (Figure 3). This model is used to verify the user's specifications and the design's viability until designing the finished product. As a result, the startup will be delivering a product that consumers like!

Startups widely use this approach to prevent the issue with the Waterfall method of getting customer input only at the end of creation. Prototyping is not a stand-alone technique. It's kind of a strategy that startups should use in conjunction with another technique to boost project performance.


## Advantages include:

- Increases the probability of product adoption by including users in the production process.

- The software's functional processes are precisely defined and analyzed.

- Reduces the likelihood of device failure.

- Requirements may be applied at any time during the production cycle.

- Identifies errors early in the production process.

- Fast customer feedback is possible, resulting in better solutions.

- Identifying missed features is easy.

Contrary to popular belief, there are a number of disadvantages of using this method.

- Prices rise as a result of changes made during the construction period.

- Excessive client participation will extend the project's duration.

• A large number of modifications have an effect on the software's workflow.

• As the scale of the construction project increases, the project complexity can shift.

**For the following situations, it is suggested:**

• Where the product specifications aren't apparent

• Where the production program must communicate with the end users often (i.e. online systems and web interfaces)

**Model V**

The V-model is ideally designed for startups with projects that have well-defined, well-understood criteria that will not change during the project. Early in the production phase, many highly technical participants are expected to perform verification and validation work.

The V-model, or Verification and Validation model, extends the waterfall model by simultaneously performing construction and verification phases (Figure 4). Parallel to the development of the software product's specifications, startups validate and incorporate them into the finished product. This enables startups to step away from abstract concepts like "user friendly" and into more realistic and verifiable criteria.

## Advantages include:

• Consists of a series of steps that team members should follow and understand.

• Prioritizes verification and evaluation early in the manufacturing process, increasing the likelihood of a quality product.

• Is a well-structured model of stages that must be completed in order.

• To make monitoring simpler, each step has its own set of deliverables and evaluation mechanisms.

• It entails proactive flaw inspection.

• Suitable for major contracts involving various staff, vendors, and subcontractors

• Project managers will reliably monitor the project's success.

Contrary to popular belief, there are a number of disadvantages of using this method.

• For lengthy contracts, increased verification work is not recommended due to the risk of schedule delays.

• The approach is not appropriate for complex and object-oriented designs when specifications are not completely implemented throughout the implementation process.

• During the planning phase, requirements cannot be changed.

• After the app has reached the testing level, it is impossible to make changes to the features.

• Late in the manufacturing period, creates a sample

• Has a hard time dealing with many incidents at the same time.

**For the following situations, it is suggested:**

• Software that offers back-end services or serves as a tool to other programs.

- Small programs with well specified and set conditions

- When SMEs on your staff are freely available to assist with the project

## Model of rapid application growth (RAD)

The accelerated application development model is ideally designed for startups with programs that must be completed quickly. To thrive, this paradigm is heavily reliant on the team's technical skills and teamwork activities.

The Rapid Application Development (RAD) model is intended to make a startup's development process more realistic by emphasizing the end-involvement. user's (Figure 5). Prototyping is used in this approach to allow for iterative growth. Via stakeholder engagement, it also fosters a collaborative environment. Long, drawn-out production and testing processes are used to complete prototyping cycles.

## Advantages include:

- Encourages and prioritizes customer reviews in order to better.

- Rather than the project manager making decisions, the functional team now does so.

- A device that is adaptable to changing requirements

- Increases the efficiency of the evaluation period

- Cuts down on construction time

- Increases productivity by reducing the number of workers involved.

- Integration is built into the project from the start.

Contrary to popular belief, there are a number of disadvantages of using this method.

- The model's performance is highly reliant on the squad.

- Handling the model's nuances necessitates highly qualified staff.

- It's not a good idea to use it for low-budget programs.

• Good team coordination is needed.

• Due to the short processing time, it is not ideal for big groups.

• Only suitable for projects with a short production period.

• Creates a difficult-to-manage dynamic production process

• Designs must be modularized in order for process phases to be completed quickly.


For the following situations, it is suggested:

• It's best for applications that gives the user a visual interface.

• When you have a group of consumers who can consistently and reliably provide input

• When you have a close deadline to deliver the commodity

**Spiral model**

Key Takeaway: The Spiral model is ideally fit for startups with projects that are high risk, and will need regular upgrades if open to customers. This model is dynamic and allows all team members to follow it to ensure success strictly.

**Advantages include:**

• Reduces damage with early detection and prevention to mitigate later cost rises

• Suitable for use during massive and complicated programs

• Allows for new conditions to be added later

• Suitable for high risk programs with diverse market requirements

• Integrating the consumer into the early stages of growth helps them to have usable input and improves their satisfaction

• Development is swift and features are added in a structured way

Contrary to popular belief, there are a number of disadvantages of using this method.

• Complex architecture model that allows developers to implement it strictly to ensure performance

• Time management is impossible to schedule when the number of stages at the outset of the project is uncertain

• Is an expensive form of app creation

• Failure during the risk analysis stage of production could harm the entire project

• Not ideal for low-risk programs

• No definite conclusion of the project, so it could continually extend and never achieve completion

• Requires agile management that may not be present within the enterprise already

For the following situations, it is suggested:

• Software that offers back-end services or serves as a tool to other programs.

- Project that needs regular releases

- Medium and high-risk programs

- Project that involves a prototype

- Requirements are vague and nuanced, and adjustments can occur at any time

- When long term project dedication is not possible due to shifts in economic preferences

**Agile product creation methodologies**

Key Takeaway: Agile software methodologies allow for versatility during development and greater user engagement. The most common agile approach for startups is the Scrum model.

Agile product development methodologies rely on community development. Stakeholders and users actively guide the development of the product together.

Startups usually use these approaches because of their lean principles. Agile methodologies eliminate excessive effort and needless paperwork. The less time you are grinding away on paperwork, the more time you will spend designing your tech app!

These methodologies agree that complexity is a part of software creation and attempting to manage improvements is difficult.

Agile software creation methodologies are widely used on projects that are:

• Low budget (less than $200 thousand), allowing startups to be agile in their strategy in an attempt to save capital

• Made up of a team of fewer than ten people

• Conducted by businesses with fewer than 250 workers

Agile approaches are certainly the hardest to pursue as a startup, as expensive errors will lead to company loss or financial disaster.

**Advantages include:**

• Ability to quickly and flexibly react to change

- Minimal systematic structures

- Communication amongst project team members is promoted

- Customer input is given during the entire production process

- Development is split into short bursts with regular product releases

Contrary to popular belief, there are a number of disadvantages of using this method.

- Highly contingent upon the inspiration and skills of the developers

- Difficult for potential team members to join the project

- Need strong listening skills to communicate with the customer consistently

- Difficult to use during major programs due to the reliance on real-time connectivity

There are several agile software methodologies available, each allowing for varying degrees of versatility during development. Understanding the most suitable agile approach for your startup's project is critical. Through knowing these models, you will be able to choose the approach that is most appropriate for your startup's mission, and preferred reaction type.

The following section discusses the core agile methodologies available and starts with the most applicable to startups, the Scrum model.

Scrum model Key Takeaway: It is best suited for startups with projects that change frequently. This model has a lengthy project lifecycle that necessitates the use of technical experts rather than novices.

One of the most vastly used agile software development approaches by startups is the scrum model. The model is based on the assumption that the development process is unpredictably unpredictable, and that requirements can (and should) change throughout the process.

This model can be used by startups to develop software quickly through a series of iterations. To ensure that development is tracked and controlled, daily scrum meetings are held that the user can attend.

**Advantages include:**

• The development team is in charge of making decisions.

• Reduces the amount of paperwork required

• Breaks down large projects into smaller chunks, allowing each component to be organized as a scrum of scrums.

• Testing is done all along the way to ensure a high-quality product.


Contrary to popular belief, there are a number of disadvantages of using this method.

• Extensive resources are required due to daily scrum meetings and frequent reviews.

• Unsuitable for large projects requiring the collaboration of multiple teams. If more than one team is needed, the project should be divided into smaller scrums to allow for easier decision-making within the team.

• Requires a team of experts; newcomers to the field will find it difficult to keep up with the fast pace.

• Long project cycle due to frequent changes, product uncertainty, and product delivery on a regular basis

• Teamwork necessitates a high level of communication.

For the following situations, it is suggested:

• It's ideal for small to medium projects.

• End-user software with a graphical user interface

• Project teams that are experienced and committed to the product

Model for lean agile software development

The lean development model is appropriate for startups with low-budget projects and short deadlines, as it allows for increased productivity. This model relies on the team's technical knowledge and collaboration efforts to succeed and maintain focus during the project.

The Lean Development methodology focuses on producing easy-to-manage software in about a third of the time. This is accomplished by limiting the budget and eliminating waste in startups. That is, your team does not create features that do not affect the final product's functionality.

This is done so that your product can be delivered quickly and with minimal functionality. Short iterations throughout the process allow for user communication and the flexibility to adapt to any unexpected risks.

Software development using the lean development model.

Advantages include:

• Reduces the project's budget and time requirements, resulting in increased efficiency.

• Delivers the final product ahead of schedule

• Increase team empowerment and motivation by involving team members in decision-making.

Contrary to popular belief, there are a number of disadvantages of using this method.

• Relies on the development team's cohesion and commitment.

• Requires members of the team to have complementary technical skills.

• Excessive flexibility causes a loss of focus.

• The software requirements must be known at the start of the process and cannot be changed later.

For the following situations, it is suggested:

• End-user software with a graphical user interface

• Short-term projects with a small budget

• Projects with fewer complications

• Projects in which the user would like to be a part of the development process

The Extreme Programming (XP) model is ideally designed for startups with open office space because it allows for quick coordination and teamwork between pairs of people on the team. To thrive, this paradigm is heavily reliant on the team's technical skills and teamwork activities.

Startups that follow the Extreme Programming (XP) paradigm build in tiny increments (Figure 9). This enables entrepreneurs to respond to changing requirements while minimizing costs rapidly.

Developers function in pairs on a basic specification and iterate on the code in response to user input. This is achieved in a clear manner such that the code can be understood and improved by all. When team members are not around to code the functionality themselves, this model helps to save time and avoid delays. Inside software development, XP is regarded as the most agile approach possible.

**Advantages include:**

• Consumers test functions to ensure that they are working properly.

• Avoids large-scale schemes by breaking them down into smaller ones.

• Increases developer motivation by including financial incentives for the implementation of specific working features.

• Eliminates production bottlenecks caused by developers operating in pairs.

• As a result of organizational cooperation, information exchange within the team increases.

Contrary to popular belief, there are a number of disadvantages of using this method.

• Open office space is needed.

• Due to the team size needed, mainly works on small to medium set tasks.

• There is no initial design step, which could result in higher costs in the future if new, incompatible standards emerge.

• The project's effectiveness is determined by the people concerned.

• Requires regular (virtual or in-person) interactions with the customer, which can be expensive or time-consuming.

For the following situations, it is suggested:

• End-user software with a graphical user interface

- Limited ventures and small teams working closely together to allow for face-to-face meetings

- Projects requiring emerging technologies, since this approach is capable of dealing with constantly evolving and technological specifications.

- Teams of which the customer is now a member

## Crystallographic techniques

The crystal approaches are ideally designed for startups and initiatives involving several teams working together to create a product quickly. Since there are too many crystal methods to choose from, there might be some inconsistency during the project when the crystal approach chosen changes as the team grows.

The Crystal Methods are a collection of color-coded software creation methodologies to indicate the potential for human life to be endangered (Figure 10). Crystal sapphire is used for projects that could pose a threat to human life, while crystal clear is used for projects that do not pose such a threat.

These approaches are common with startups because they are known to be very adaptable. Since they are structured as a human-centric project rather than a product- or business-centric project, this is the case.

Because of the number of team members and the project's atmosphere, startups preferred the color of the crystal process. When it comes to designing a tech app, the most widely used crystal creation approach for startups is Crystal Clear.

**Advantages include:**

• Ensures regular deliverables to recognise potential issues at - point

• Enhances features by encouraging dialogue on ways to improve the operation.

• Facilitates enhanced collaboration and information sharing among team members.

• A technological infrastructure with automatic checks, configuration management, and regular testing is needed.

• Every week, a reflection session is held to ensure consistent communication about the creation process.

• Isn't mutually exclusive for other approaches.

Contrary to popular belief, there are a number of disadvantages of using this method.

• Designs that are difficult to complete due to the large variety of crystal methods available. The concepts of each approach change depending on the size of the team and the scope of the project.

• Managing physically dispersed teams is daunting due to the ongoing need to collaborate and reflect.

• Significant resources are being dedicated to regular meetings and improved team/user collaboration. This diverts attention away from construction efforts.

• User participation is achieved only for staggered updates, rather than during the implementation process.

• There are no conditions for planning and construction.

For the following situations, it is suggested:

• Organizations with a high level of internal coordination.

• Projects with pre-determined team sizes that would not adjust during production

- Projects that are not concerned with the user experience

## Model for the growth of dynamic systems (DSDM)

The dynamic machine architecture model is ideally fit for startups working on projects with set funding and deadlines. This model lacks established practices for dealing with a project's scalability later in the development process.

The Rapid Application Development (RAD) paradigm is used to create the Dynamic System Development Model (DSDM). The methodology is iterative and gradual, emphasizing the user's presence in the implementation process (Figure 11).

This is a good model for entrepreneurs because it needs fixed costs and time, which you might be dealing with right now. As a consequence, in order to meet the timetable, functionality specifications are updated. This model is set up in such a way that the production process takes the least amount of time available and that each delivery includes the majority of the specifications.

**Advantages include:**

• Provides simple product features quickly.

• User testing during implementation improves customers' comprehension of the product.

• Developers have easy access to consumers.

• Consistently complete assignments on schedule

•Contrary to popular belief, there are a number of disadvantages of using this method.

• Implementation is expensive.

• Due to the expected fast turnaround, this service is not ideal for small businesses.

• There are no defined procedures for dealing with the project's scalability.

• At the outset of the process, the requirements are vague.

• Represents a significant and transformative shift in the company's philosophy.

For the following situations, it is suggested:

• For businesses that emphasize rapid development when performing on schedule and on budget.

• Projects with set budgets and deadlines

• Products that need to hit the market as soon as possible

Key Takeaway: The feature guided development (FDD) paradigm is ideally designed for startups that have projects with several teams working together to create a product quickly. This model is not suitable for a single developer, and it necessitates the involvement of lead developers who can closely track feature creation.

The Feature Driven Development (FDD) paradigm is based on the creation of features. There are tiny, well-defined programs within a broader project (Figure 12).

FDD specializes in dealing with organizations who have several teams collaborating on a project using object-oriented programming. This is a common agile approach among startups because of its multi-team structure.

To ensure the functions are introduced to the user easily, the FDD model employs short-iteration methods (e.g. every two weeks a new feature is presented). As a consequence, startups prioritize the most critical user experiences.

**Advantages include:**

• The five-step mechanism allows for accelerated growth.

• Makes use of pre-defined production guidelines to enable teams to work rapidly.

• Enables larger teams to drive goods forward successfully.

• Scalable to large-scale programs

• Allows for the delivery of concrete data after two weeks.

Contrary to popular belief, there are a number of disadvantages of using this method.

• Due to the expected fast turnaround, this service is not ideal for small businesses.

• Relies on the lead developers so the mechanism must be monitored at all times.

• Requires the customer to provide functionality that are specifically defined and prioritized.

• Causes ambiguity due to a lack of paperwork

For the following situations, it is suggested:

• Large corporations engaged in research and development

• Programs including large-scale software creation

• Organizations with a top-down decision-making mechanism

## What do you look for when choosing a software creation methodology?

The decision on which software development approach to use is an important step in the development process. Until settling on a growth approach, make sure the startup analyses corporate, mission, and team characteristics.

When it comes to starting a tech startup, choosing a software creation approach is crucial. This technique must be chosen and followed from start to finish by your startup.

It's difficult to change the model halfway through the process. Changing the procedure confuses everyone on the team, potentially delaying progress. This is particularly not recommended for startups due to the financial and time implications of changing methodologies.

Many business experts agree that the most common cause of project loss is the use of an ineffective construction process. The product could not be completed on schedule or under budget, resulting in project loss. It might even fail if the consumer isn't getting anything out of it.

Assess various concept models in light of corporate, mission, and team characteristics. This eliminates the possibility of literature or other people's advice biassing your startup choices.

Characteristics to consider when choosing a software development approach

By concentrating on your project's unique scenario, your startup will make a fantastic product. The following are important characteristics to consider before deciding on a production methodology:

**Personalities of the community**

• Team size – Use an approach that has been shown to work for a team of the same size as yours.

• Team positions – Depending on the organizational framework within the startup, teams can have members of several specific roles (e.g. project manager, engineers, planner, technical facilitator, etc.) can include a more formal approach.

• Project expertise – Agile methodologies require highly skilled team members, while conventional methodologies will effectively involve inexperienced developers. Examine the production team to see what the percentage of different ability levels is. Don't hesitate to assess the executive team's expertise to ensure that they can effectively handle a more agile project framework.

• Business management style – If the startup is run top-down, team decision-making would be impossible, stopping any agile growth approaches from achieving their maximum potential.

## Specifications of the project

• Project scale – Certain methodologies are designed to operate exclusively on small tasks with a short processing time.

• Project sophistication – Dynamic projects necessitate a more flexible planning approach to allow for adaptation to any problems that occur through development.

• Project risk – Owing to the predictable intervals of customer reviews, agile product development methodologies are ideally designed for high-risk programs.

• Project budget – If necessary, choose a methodology that focuses on remaining under budget rather than methodologies that allow for greater flexibility, as this would typically increase the project's expense.

• Design specifications – Under traditional methodologies, the software requirements must be understood before the project begins. More agile development approaches allow startups to alter specifications during the development process quickly.

• Number of necessary reviews – A conventional approach is ineffective if the startup requires a lot of customer input during the implementation phase. The customer is normally not given a product to study until it is thoroughly established in standard methodologies.

**Communication is important.**

• The team's geographical position – Certain methodologies necessitate regular contact with team members. This can be daunting if the startup is dispersed around multiple job centers, let alone across multiple geographical regions.

• Customer usability – The chosen technique can necessitate constant consumer input. You must ensure that your startup has customers who are willing and ready to provide you with input.

**Factors affecting the project from outside**

• Demand stability – If the market for your consumer platform is continuously changing, you can use a more agile approach. This will give you more options throughout the production process.

• Market standards – Standard methodologies can be best suited if the industry the product would join needs strict obedience to regulations. This is due to the large volume of paperwork that must be completed.

• Quality assurance protocol in effect – An agile product development process is appropriate if the startup has a professionally defined Quality Assurance (QA) scheme. This is because a fully integrated QA framework provides for constant checking to ensure that the product provided at the end of production is fully functional and validated.

# Chapter 4 Project Management in the DSDM

## Roles and Responsibilities of DSDM Project Management

### CATEGORIES OF ROLES

Within DSDM, the functions are classified into three levels or divisions. The Project Level, the Solution Development Team, and the Support-Related Positions are the three categories. The Project Level and the Solution Development Team comprise your main Project Team.

### Level of the Project

Within their specialization or region, Project Level positions are responsible for directing and/or overseeing aspects of the project. Interacting with stakeholders and providing project governance will be the responsibilities of roles at the project level. They have the project's required vision and work to ensure that the vision is carried out.

## Team in charge of developing solutions

The Solution Development Team (SDT) is in charge of getting the vision to reality. They collaborate to create the project's proposed product. People assigned to these positions should not be changed out or replaced as far as possible. The aim is to provide a secure SDT that takes responsibility for their work and responsibilities.

## Supporting Characters

When required, Supporting Roles include project direction. They can work on different projects or serve in other capacities within the company. In a project, their function is to advise or assist the Solution Development Team in their field of expertise.

## THE RESPONSIBILITIES AND ROLES

The DSDM functions are color-coded according to their primary function or form.

The functions involved in managing or envisioning the business's priorities are represented by orange.

Green positions are people that work around electronics or contribute to the project's strategic solution.

The Team Leader and the Project Manager are the only blue positions for the project's leadership.

Gray positions are those that are responsible for ensuring that DSDM activities are understood and followed.

## Sponsorship by a business

The Company Sponsor is a senior business role on a project. The Corporate Sponsor serves as the project's champion and is in charge of the project's business case and budget. Owing to the need to make management and financial decisions, this role demands a higher degree of authority within the company. The Program Manager could fill this position if the project is part of a DSDM program.

A committee may fill the Business Sponsor position on larger and more complicated programs. In this position, the organization should only have one individual or a unified committee/board. Where opposed to seeing many individual individuals attempt to play this position, this helps have a smoother course of escalation of problems and decreases tension.

**Responsibilities include:**

• Keeping the project's Business Case up to date

• Financial oversight of the project

• Establishing efficient decision-making procedures

• Dealing with escalating disputes

• Enabling everyone in the market to do their best work

• Being conscious and involved with the project's progress and continuing work.

**Entrepreneurial Thinker**

The Corporate Visionary interprets the company's desires and communicates the company's vision to the project team. They are required to have a consistent, straightforward vision for the project during its lifetime. The Business Change Owner role may fill the Business Visionary position within DSDM program management if the project is part of a program.

Responsibilities: • Provide the business vision and explain that to the team and other stakeholders • Resolve conflicts related to the business vision

- Ensure that the project's success remains in line with the company's goals.

- Assist with the interpretation of project adjustment demands

- Participate in concept and analysis workshops including the company vision.

- Assist the initiative with corporate tools

- Serve as a servant leader to the project's corporate positions.


## Coordinator of Technical Services

The project's technical authority, the Technical Coordinator, ensures that technical operations are planned and managed. They will have the project's technological vision and strive to ensure that it is in line with the company vision. The Program Technical Architect can fill the position of Technical Coordinator in a DSDM program.

**Responsibilities include:**

- Managing the project's technological architecture

- Organizing and coordinating technical exercises

- Providing advice on the viability of technological proposals

- Considering technological alternatives to achieve the company's goals

- Ensuring adherence to professional best practices

- Managing the transition from an established to a published state of the solution

- Using servant leadership to empower professional mission positions

- Resolve disagreements over technical decisions

## Manager of the project

The Project Manager is in charge of supplying the team with "Agile-style leadership." As a result, rather than being an authoritative boss, the Project Manager in DSDM is something like a servant or facilitative leader. The Project Manager is in charge of coordinating and empowering the whole team and putting the puzzle pieces together.

**Responsibilities include:**

- Ensure the feedback is timely and accurate.

- Strategic strategy

- Working with partners to develop a delivery strategy

- Keep track of the project's success.

- Resolve and manage threats

- Inspire and encourage the team

- Deal with escalating issues

## Business Analyst

The Business Analyst is part of the Solution Development Team who supports Project Level positions. They are an intermediary between the Project Level and the SDT. They promote the production of the solution by leading the SDT to make acceptable decisions within the solution development.

## Responsibilities include:

- Assist the Company Visionary in the advancement of the business vision

- Identify potential threats and impacts on the execution of the solution

- Assist Project Level in business case development

- facilitate contact as required

- **Ensure standards are properly specified and achievable**

### Ambassador for Business

Within the Solution Development Team, the Business Ambassador represents the business needs. During Evolutionary Development, they provide daily requirements to the team and are the business's primary decision-maker.

### Responsibilities include:

- Participate in sessions on requirements, design, and review.

- Provide a business perspective for decision-making by solution teams.

- In charge of the solution's documentation as well as support documentation.

• Ensuring that users are properly trained on how to use the solution

## Developer of solutions

The Solution Developer converts business requirements into a Solution Increment that satisfies the increment's requirements. This includes all of the roles that are required to complete the solution or a portion of the solution. To help reduce risk and waste, this should be a full-time position dedicated solely to the project.

## Responsibilities include:

• Working together to develop a solution increment each iteration

• Complying with technical constraints and the organization's development standards

• Assist with quality assurance

## Solution Examiner

The Solution Tester's job is to ensure that the solution works and that it meets the agreed-upon standards.

## Responsibilities include:

• Define the testing requirements and test case scenarios.

• Test each solution increment as well as the entire solution.

• Keep track of testing activities and quality issues and report them.

## Business Consultant

The Business Advisor's job is to make sure that the solution's testing meets the company's needs. They could be a Subject Matter Expert and/or a potential solution user or provide regulatory and legal advice. They provide more direct and detailed business advice on the solution.

**Responsibilities include:**

• Contribute expert knowledge to the solution

**Advisor on technical matters**

The Technical Advisor assists with the solution's technical aspects. They could be in charge of making operational changes, assisting with the release, or maintaining the solution.

**Responsibilities include:**

• Examine the technical specifications and offer specialized advice

• Conduct acceptance testing in the field

• Provide technical operations and support staff with training.

**Facilitator of Workshops**

The workshop process will be managed by the Workshop Facilitator. They are in charge of planning meetings that achieve a workshop goal.

**Responsibilities include:**

• Working with the workshop owner to agree on the workshop's scope and facilitating the workshop

## What is the DSDM Agile Project Framework, and how does it work?

The DSDM Agile Project Framework is one of the most popular and effective Agile project management frameworks. DSDM (Dynamic Systems Development Method) is an Agile method that focuses on the entire project life cycle. It was created in 1994 after project managers using RAD (Rapid Application Development) felt the need for more government and discipline for the new iterative form of work that was taking hold. Its eight guiding principles are as follows:

1. Concentrate on the business requirement.

2. Meet deadlines.

3. Work together.

4. Never scrimp on quality.

5. Begin with a solid foundation and work your way up.

6. Work iteratively.

7. Maintain constant and clear communication.

8. Show that you're in command.

**What is the significance of this?**

The framework is based on the belief that every project should be clearly aligned with an organization's strategic objectives and focused on quickly delivering real value. It covers the whole project life cycle and offers best practices for completing projects on time, on budget, and with proven scalability in any business sector.

## Practices in Agile Management and Procurement

The Agile Manifesto prioritizes customer collaboration over contract negotiation, setting an important tone for agile project procurement relationships. The Agile Manifesto establishes the concept of a buyer and seller cooperating to create products and governs the entire procurement process.

The agile management approach to determining need and selecting a vendor

Procurement on agile projects begins when the development team determines that it requires a tool or another company's services to complete the project. The development team and scrum master collaborate with the product owner to secure any funds that are required.

The development team may have to compare tools and vendors. After you've decided what you want to buy and where you'll get it, the process is usually simple: make the purchase, accept delivery, and the procurement is finished.

Purchasing services takes longer and is more complicated than purchasing tools. The following are some agile-specific considerations for selecting a services vendor:

• Is the vendor capable of working in an agile project environment, and if so, how much experience does he or she have?

• Is the vendor willing to collaborate with the development team on-site?

• Is the vendor's relationship with the scrum team likely to be positive and collaborative?

The agile management approach to contracts and cost approaches for services

To begin the contracting process, you must first understand various pricing structures and how they interact with agile projects.

Cost structures for an agile project are being evaluated.

To fairly assess value, you must be aware of various cost structures:

• Fixed-price projects: A vendor works on the product and creates releases until the budget is depleted or until enough product features are delivered, whichever comes first.

• Projects with a set start and end date: For example, you may need to launch a product in time for a specific event or coincide with another product launch. With fixed-time projects, you calculate costs based on the vendor's team's salary for the duration of the project and any additional resource costs, such as hardware or software.

• Time-and-materials projects: Work with the vendor continues until sufficient product functionality is achieved, regardless of the overall project cost. After your stakeholders determine that the product has enough features to call the project complete, you'll know the total project cost.

• Projects with a fixed-price cap on time and materials are known as not-to-exceed projects.

## Creating a contract for a project that is agile

The scrum master is in charge of initiating contract creation, negotiating contract details, and routing the contract through any internal approvals that are required, including review by a legal or procurement expert.

Most contracts include legal language that describes the parties and the work and the budget, cost approach, and payment terms. A contract for an agile project may also include the following clauses:

• A description of the work to be done by the vendor: The vendor may have its own product vision statement, which can serve as a good starting point for describing the vendor's work.

• The vendor may use agile approaches such as:

o Meetings in which the vendor will participate, such as daily scrums, sprint planning, sprint review, and sprint retrospective

o At the end of each sprint, deliver working functionality

o Per an agreement between the product owner and the development team, the definition of done is developed, tested, integrated, and documented.

o Deliverables from the vendor, such as a sprint backlog with a burndown chart

o People who will be working on the project with the vendor, such as the development team

o Is the vendor willing to work on-site?

o Whether the vendor will collaborate with its own scrum master and product owner or with your own scrum master and product owner.

o A definition of what constitutes the end of the engagement: the expiration of a fixed budget or time limit, or the completion of sufficient working functionality

• Even if the vendor is unable to work on-site at the buyer's facility, it can still be a member of the buyer's scrum team. If a vendor cannot be collocated with the buyer's scrum team, or if the vendor is responsible for a discrete, separate part of the product, the vendor may have its own scrum team working on the same sprint schedule.

• If a vendor does not use agile project management processes, the vendor's team works outside of the sprints and on its own schedule, separate from the buyer's scrum team. The traditional project manager for the vendor ensures that the vendor's services are available when the development team requires them. If the vendor's processes or timeline become a roadblock or disruption for the development team, the buyer's scrum master may need to intervene.

• Signing a contract for a project involving agile management.

• When a vendor completes work on a contract, the buyer's scrum master usually has a few last tasks to complete.

• If the project is finished according to the contract's terms, the scrum master may write a written acknowledgment of the contract's end. If the project is a time-and-materials project, the scrum master should immediately ensure that the vendor does not continue to work on lower-priority requirements and bill for them.

• The scrum master may be in charge of informing the buyer's accounting department so that the vendor is properly paid.

• If the project is completed before the contract expires, the scrum master must notify the vendor in writing and follow any contract early termination instructions.

## Agile Project Management Challenges and Solutions

### 1. Getting into a squabble with the finance department.

Every move isn't explained in extreme depth and mapped out in an agile mentality and project management strategy. This is a significant shift for many finance divisions, which have a more conservative and prudent approach. One of the major obstacles that a company faces as it becomes agile is funding and finance.

Traditionally, an organization must prepare a business case for a project that included the project's reach as well as a completely costed platform down to the last penny. "In agile ventures, there is extra space to maneuver, update, and turn stuff around," says Ken Gains, a project manager at State of Writing and Ox Essays. All isn't meticulously prepared and costed to the last cent. Finance agencies have a hard time with that."

Organizations require accountability and a realignment of finance and other agencies to address this problem so that they can work more closely together and appreciate what's going on. Finance must be brought on board by the company and operating departments, and that can help to understand why many commonly costed programs are often late and over-budget. When finance departments are confronted with these facts, they are more likely to be open to reform.

## 2. For some people, less preparation can be difficult.

Before committing to greenlight a proposal, many business executives want a comprehensive plan of the project's benefits and the projected net cost. Many leaders believe that understanding how much a project would cost just when it is completed, or just performing the next job that needs to be finished without a schedule, is insufficient.

Leaders must follow a more agile approach and recognize that agile programs also need planning, but in a different way. It is perfectly appropriate to plan in the context of criteria scoping, construction work, and project architecture, as well as time and money forecasts for sprints and stages. If achieved in sprints, agile will require preparation and continuous adaptation.

### 3. Aversion to transition.

The most difficult task is likely to transform the whole company's attitude and culture, as some people are often resistant to change, particularly one as significant as being agile. A fascinating fact is that 61% of people who have adopted agile strategies believe that businesses should prioritize their people and business culture as a primary priority for change management.

At the end of the day, no matter what new systems are introduced and evaluated, agile businesses need a paradigm shift in how workers learn about and approach their jobs. Company executives must take a pragmatic approach to the change, demonstrating the value of an agile approach and providing adequate preparation and support for staff to realize how the transformation can operate and why it is necessary. Leaders must adapt and lead by example, by being honest and soliciting input and dialogue from their teams. They should also allow their teams to synchronize on a regular basis so that everyone is on the same page.

## 4. Conventional HR procedures.

HR agencies may benefit from agile practices when it comes to hiring, assessing, and rewarding staff. Agile is a positive way of operating and it ensures that the tasks benefit from the contributions of the best individuals, rather than obsolete job requirements or specific positions. Individuals will move forward because they are confident and skilled in the project's area, because they have collaborated with coworkers who are equally enthusiastic about the project.

These individuals benefit the project because they are motivated by an exciting project or task and the opportunity to collaborate for a new team or leader, rather than by monetary rewards or advantages. To address the needs of team-based growth, agile organizations should update their incentive and success schemes.


## 5. Using the waterfall method.

Any companies implement agile in the wrong way, using a core and in-depth strategy (the waterfall mindset), which causes rollouts to slow. Starting with minor adjustments and keeping the ball rolling, understanding and improving the strategy as they go is the perfect way to move to an agile enterprise.

Employee burnout is a problem of agile transitions as workers spend too much time early in the process and don't pace themselves out for the long haul. When a project begins, team members will overestimate their skills, forcing them to work long hours and overtime to meet their deadlines. As a result, team members struggle, make mistakes, and have low morale. As a consequence, the project fails, and no one in the organization benefits. The squad, which began strong and positive, becomes tense and resentful, and cracks appear.

Finally, both of these factors contribute to increased failures, team member abandonment, and project loss. To stop agile burnout, business owners should recruit agile facilitators, also known as scrum masters, who can ensure that agile teams have accurate forecasts and that things move forward at a reasonable speed for all.

Pre-existing challenges in an organization, such as regulatory departments and outdated processes that can't support fast project iterations, can influence how agile project management is implemented. Around the same time as implementing agile methodologies, businesses must change their practices and structures.

Agile projects are very popular, but it is not enough to apply the agile approach to all projects. Anything that necessitates the involvement of third parties or the incorporation of several departments that do not always use agile in the same way should be handled more conventionally. There's a possibility that if an enterprise has completed agile projects, everybody tries to do agile projects on any project, but if done incorrectly, the effects may be disastrous for the business.

Each project can be evaluated separately to ensure that the agile approach is the right fit for it. "Agile is better applicable when the solution is complicated or uncertain, and when the task will progress over several rapid iterations," says Sandra Thatcher, a team leader at Paper Fellows and Boom Essays. Organizations that use diverse methods for different programs are the most successful."

Brand owners, scrum masters, and agile team managers all have various positions in agile programs. There should be certain specialized tasks, such as checking and coordination, but if teams are left to determine these roles, performance will suffer and the team will not perform as well as it should.

Any business executives are tempted to become agile only because it is a recent development in many sectors. Suppose an organization adopts agile simply for the sake of doing so without considering whether it is the right option for them. In that case, they will find that their competitiveness suffers and that consumer loyalty suffers as a result. If agility is a crucial result, the strategy should be updated to include more realistic market objectives.

## Keys to Effective Agile Methodologies Implementation

### 1. Begin with the proper project.

While agile methodologies can be applied to virtually any kind of project, efficient application of these techniques necessitates choosing the right projects to begin with to gain the most value in the shortest amount of time.

Attempting to adapt agile methodologies to explicitly predictable or classic programs seldom yields positive outcomes and there is a significant fear of losing leverage, with teams (and management) reverting to approaches they are familiar with. On the other hand, experimental programs with a less developed or extremely changeable nature, multidisciplinary teams, and a need for quick performance are an ideal fit for agile methodologies.

### 2. Describe the team's function in detail.

A team's position in traditional or predictive projects differs greatly from their role in agile projects. In the former, the Project Manager is in charge of all facets of the project, while in the latter, the team is even more important and the Project Manager becomes a facilitator of the methodology. In order to accurately execute the process, it is critical to identify the team's position clearly.

A multidisciplinary, self-organized, and self-directed team is required for an agile project, which poses a trust challenge for those organizations that choose to use managed and regulated approaches. It is critical to comprehend and construct this sort of team. A significant portion of your potential progress can be assured if you can form a team that consists of relationships between a common purpose and equals.

### 3. Estimation of Effort Remains Crucial

When applying agile methodologies, one of the most common issues is the belief that forecasts are no longer necessary. Even if it is no longer possible to quantify the whole project and we can concentrate on the tasks for the next sprint or those with a higher priority in the product backlog, it is critical to realistically estimate the effort needed for the tasks to ensure that they are equally comparable or that the size discrepancy between them is obvious.

Suppose a task is not finished at the end of a sprint or is often marked as "ongoing" in a Kanban project. In that case, it is most possible that we made a calculation error that needs to be resolved, the task should be broken down into more manageable bits, and our obligations should be updated often. Flexible management can ensure that the estimate reflects on the projects of the greatest priority or that we must complete as soon as possible. The calculation, on the other hand, is also crucial.

## 4. Recognize and manage limitations

Agile methodologies have their own set of constraints that must be considered. Scope, deadline, expense, and consistency are all considerations that must be met. Real, targets may be reversed or the spectrum may be more negotiable, but deadlines, costs, and efficiency constraints also exist and must be handled.

These strategies say that projects do not take more than a given amount of time, determine a maximum Work in Progress (WIP) that we can handle, and use sprints to set a time limit. Since limitations are such an integral aspect of their model, they must be strictly adhered to and not modified lightly. We lose direction as we make modifications or revisions and welcome all kinds of improvements.

## 5. Deal with tense situations

Agile methodologies, contrary to popular belief, are more akin to a marathon than a run. Some companies use these strategies to move more efficiently – to get more accomplished with less time – by using the reality that teams are more closely involved. True, but if we want these strategies to stick, we need to handle team friction.

Agile approach makes it easy to provide a driven, results-oriented, self-managed, and effective team. To ensure that these qualities last over time, we must ensure that the team has a boost in productivity rather than a relentless increase in commitment and workload.

## 6. Metrics: "Power is worthless without control."

These techniques are highly effective. They have the ability to create driven teams that produce amazing results in a very short period. All of this force, though, does not come at the expense of control. Agile methodologies allow us to calculate, assess, and develop our work on a regular basis.

Metrics are the path to explicit project management focused on actual metrics rather than intuition, beliefs, or the occurrence of unforeseen events. In order to streamline our processes and strengthen our teams, we can collect and review key metrics such as speed, flow, and engagement enforcement.


## 7. Quality

The repeat market is based on quality. Increasing execution rates, incrementally handling forecasts, or providing a self-managed team does not imply sacrificing efficiency. Agile methodologies are critical to producing goods fast, but those products must also work; they must do what is demanded of them effectively.

That is why it is critical not to leave quality until the end of the project and to provide elements of quality confirmation, revision, and measurement of all objects, deliverables, and goods from the start.

## 8. Stick to the technique as closely as possible.

There are few guidelines, principles, or goods in agile methodologies. It's crucial to stick to the approach exactly, particularly at first. Before accumulating experience, it is preferable to change nothing (or almost nothing). Have a little faith and offer something a shot if it looks different.

Scrum methods define a set of tasks, gatherings, and stages that must be retained, observed, and sustained for the methods to perform as intended. You can progress from fewer to more in these techniques, but you must follow their guidelines to the letter before you are satisfied with them.

## 9. Adapt and revise the process

We should think about making changes to agile methodologies after we've made great progress on them. Conducting evaluations or observational exercises allows you to see what works and what doesn't in your company, as well as making the requisite adjustments to tailor the approach to your history, style, and needs. This can, though, only be done after you've tested the regular ones.

Agile methodologies are very adaptable, which is why they can be applied to almost any project, organization, or team. Possible imbalances can be detected with a little practice, and improvements, modifications, or adjustments to these approaches can be made to ensure that they perfectly meet our needs and circumstances.

## 10. Increase the exposure.

Visibility is one of the most important factors in the performance of agile methodologies. At certain organizations, these techniques are implemented "behind the scenes," almost invisibly, as if using this kind of tool would be humiliating in some way. This method of execution should be made transparent, accessible, and available so that everyone in the company can see what's been implemented, how it's being done, and what's been accomplished.

When the project recipient or supporter arrives, avoid using private "Kanban" methods or covering them. Display, illustrate, and capitalize on the most obvious advantages. A project client or mentor who is interested in management is an invaluable partner, and agile methodologies allow for optimal visibility and input from all stakeholders. Agile technique isn't a one-off or an extravagance for a certain group of people; it's something that can be seen around the board.

## 11. Keep expectations in check

Many teams and companies that follow this course assume that their challenges will be fixed as if by magic; that the customer will never change their mind, that goods will no longer have flaws, and that nothing "unpleasant" will ever happen again during the process. Agile methodologies respond well to evolving and stressful situations, but they aren't a panacea for all issues. Effective execution necessitates managing demands from teams, partners, and management.

It's possible that the system won't be flawless the first time around, that teams will be dissatisfied with some facets of the method, or that the project will run into issues. This is perfectly natural doing. You'll soon see that progress is being made, that it's significant, and that the findings are very optimistic.

## 12. Choose the appropriate tools

When implementing agile methodologies, using a help tool makes them easier to incorporate in organizations. It is critical to provide centralized support for exchanging knowledge, monitoring success, and retaining project control. Teams will be able to operate individually using the right instrument, while the company will be able to keep track of project success, expenses and sales, efforts, and so on.

Don't be misled by free resources that are totally detached from the rest of the business. Agile methodologies aren't a one-off or remarkable technique used by teams with shoddy tools; they're a strategic effort made by the enterprise to change and develop. We are in the midst of a project management revolution that will enable us to boost our results, produce high-value goods faster, and achieve great success if we have the right resources.

## Keys to Putting Together a Good Agile Squad

### Inspiration

According to the report, traditional motivators such as growth, performance, and risk need to be replaced, emphasizing results and consumers as a grand target.

According to Dave West, product owner at Scrum.org, "the organization and procedures must be aligned to the client or to a collection of standards." "Clearly specified results are needed, as is intimacy with the consumer vision and a commitment to provide value for these outcomes."

Workers are often inspired by these results, according to West. "By offering them an idea of the client and the result they're looking to achieve," he says, "you will get a lot more out of the organization." "Successful teams are deeply invested in the results they provide, and individuals who excel at agile have a natural knack for this."

## WHITEPAPERS RECOMMENDED

It's critical to determine people's passions, what excites them, and where they see themselves in three years. Many who love solving difficult problems and see complexity as an ability to improve, according to the report, are more likely to succeed.

## Beliefs and expectations

It's all about coordination when it comes to agility. Successful agile teams are made up of individuals who work well together and do whatever it takes to achieve the desired results. But, as West points out, the aspirations of peers and clients and partners are often fluid and diverse. Since effective agile teams are self-directed and have a flat organizational structure, a new equilibrium between priorities and confidence must be created.

According to Wouter Aghina, a partner at McKinsey and a pioneer of McKinsey's agile company work, "mass manufacturing processes believe in a 'parental' hierarchy of management." "You have a team leader who says, 'All right, we need to build these pieces.' You'll work on X and he'll work on Y, and I'll tell you what to do.

You'll sit at your desk and do your work, and if you have a question, you can come to me and I'll answer it.' This is becoming more ineffective; it doesn't work, and it's demoralizing," he adds.

Job management and value management should be separated in agile teams, according to West.

"One of the most important reasons to do this is to build confidence and accountability, which is difficult to do because the same individual manages and incentivizes you," he says. "This type of 'servant leadership' would not be able to meet these demands while still fostering the confidence and openness that are required of good agile teams."

According to the study, it's critical to inquire into how people collaborate with one another, how they handle work as a squad, and what they want others to do in their help. You'll be able to hire candidates who can excel in the kind of atmosphere that a good agile team needs.

## A customer-focused viewpoint

Customers are engaged and their needs are learned through effective agile teams. Customers and agile teams work together to accomplish targets and identify the most cost-effective solutions in agile organizations. In typical organizations, there is typically one point of touch — one person or company — responsible for communicating with the customer; in agile organizations, customers and agile teams learn together to achieve goals and find the most cost-effective solutions.

According to the study, while a team is based on clients and using an agile strategy, it is most likely to produce value to them incrementally and regularly. Agile workers are much more driven when they understand who they are assisting. Ask questions about what they might expect as consumers and what customer service means to them to ensure you have the best people on board.

## Take care of the art.

Any part of an agile organization must be concerned with their craft and the results of their practice. Agile teams take responsibility for the products they create.

According to the study, pride in the result and results is more important to them than pride in the process.

"Understanding the nuances and ambiguities of this kind of knowledge work is one of the most daunting facets of agile for organizations going through or having been through a transformation," West says. "These models function in conventional organizations where you have well-understood challenges. These information workers and the challenges they're working on are complicated and quickly evolving, particularly in these modern, IT-driven, creative environments."

According to West, most agile teams don't know exactly what they're working on, or even what the challenge is, until they get started. Effective agile teams understand that the process can and will evolve as they evaluate the relationship between the process and the meaning and results it produces.

Ask questions about past encounters with work they're proud of, and relate those experiences to their priorities and values, as well as the organization's goals and values, to ensure team members are truly invested.

## What is an Agile Transformation Case Study, and what does it entail?

Case studies are also known as "customer accounts" or "success stories," which are primarily used in marketing. They're written with the user in mind, and they're meant to demonstrate the importance of a service. The aim isn't always to market a product or service.

Professional services companies that offer agile consultancy also use case studies as part of their marketing campaigns, with a section or segment on their website devoted solely to transition case studies. These persuasive customer stories are an excellent way to demonstrate the importance of an agile transition to a business.

The majority of studies are provided in.pdf format, which allows for fast distribution, although some companies can also have footage. LEGO Digital Solutions, for example, introduced their agile transformation insights, and Scaled Agile shared the film.

Case studies can be used for a variety of things, from delivering extra instructional content and gathering evidence for a business case for agile transformation.

If an organization is planning to implement an agile change process or technique, or is now doing so, case studies may be a valuable resource for teams and leadership. Case studies use "real-life" scenarios that certain people can react to more easily than theoretical experience.

## Case Study on Agile Transformation: What Makes a Good Case Study?

A case study can be a valuable guide for creating a solid business case for agile transition because of the analytical insights it provides.

A well-written case study should include, at a minimum, the following items mentioned in a simple, succinct format:

• Information about the company, including its industry

• A summary of the issue or decision that must be taken

• Obstacles, questions, and/or possibilities

• Alternatives

• Issues that arose during the implementation of the solution and how they were resolved

- Outcomes

Additional supporting statistics, such as installation costs, higher productivity costs, software quality measurement, return on investment, benchmarks, and financial reports, can be used to help quantify performance.

# Case Study: Barclay's Retail and Business Banking

The Barclay's Retail and Banking agile transition case study starts with the main "takeaways," presenting what they discovered as a result of agile transformation right away. The case study also includes detail about why they needed to transition, what they hoped to accomplish with agility, and the "why," "when," and "how" claims, which offer further insight into their agile transition process.

More evidence can be gathered, referenced, and analyzed as more companies engage in transition and publicize their findings through case studies. This knowledge will also help to debunk the myth that agile is only a fad.

## How CAST Will Assist

• CAST assists companies conducting agile transitions with calculation strategies. These indicators are presented in a series of audience-specific dashboards that offer insight into the management of dynamic change programs.

• Prior to implementing agile, provide a benchmark for evaluating the efficiency and effectiveness of the application development process. The baseline establishes a factual view of the current state of growth, teams, and performance in order to serve as a benchmark for future progress.

• Establish baselines for key applications based on the most critical product health criteria to ensure that they do not deteriorate through the agile transition. During the transition process, this safeguards vital systems.

• Govern and control risk and quality using management standards and benchmarks that have been developed.

• Assist with quality management by measuring the performance of the application development process in an integrated, long-term manner.

• Assess the efficiency and effectiveness of the production process after the agile transition to track progress and determine ROI.

## What is the Agile Canon, and how does it work?

The Agile Canon is a project that aims to improve the concept of agility. We'll know if it's useful if it can help us discern between good and poor agile tools, and if it can point us in the right direction for improvement.

My aim is to assist you in understanding certain trends so that you, your staff, and your company can achieve greater success.

Agile methods assist them in evaluating, experimenting, learning, adapting, and improving. Agility helps us achieve our most important goals: developing new skills, starting new companies, forming new partnerships, and meeting new obstacles.

Agile methods lead to experiments, and discoveries lead to amazing artistic results. All fascinating tasks necessitate imaginative effort; if we could simply copy what others had achieved, we'd get bored quickly. In today's information age, where mechanical labor has been streamlined, society offers little opportunities for repeating what others have done. Take a look around you: nearly everyone is working on something.

Uncertainty fosters creativity. Our most rewarding endeavors are those in which we are unsure whether or not we can succeed. The more unpredictable performance is, the more agile strategies are beneficial.

The Agile Canon is a compilation of basic agile techniques that is systematic. Manufacturing, software creation, creative production, and marketing have all been put to the test. You should employ costly coaches to assist you with learning field-specific activities such as Scrum. However, if you learn field-specific practices without first mastering the basics, your abilities can easily become insufficient in new contexts. You will build appropriate field-specific agile strategies at any time by mastering agile basics (and you will benefit more from field-specific training).

## Encourage the use of the Agile Canon

### Participate in the Agile Canon.

The Agile Canon is a work-in-progress with lofty goals. I won't be capable to do it by myself. In reality, much of this work has been reviewed several times by friends from various fields.

**You are used to**

• Create a stand-alone chapter about a practice you believe is lacking. We'll work together to incorporate it into the Canon, and you'll be given credit for that chapter. To aid in your endeavors, you may want to review How to Read and Write Pattern Languages.

• Follow a field—for example, Lean Startup, XP, or Getting Things Done—and write methods that use the Base Practices. This is a big project, so I'll pitch in and give you credit, of course.

**Become a Supporter**

And send me an email. My inspiration stems from my need to assist others. When my research and writing project aids others in their success, I am barely aware of it. People are shy or scared, but I treasure notes from strangers; they give meaning to my life. If everything goes well because you read the Agile Canon, please send me a thank-you message.

Consider being a Patreon patron supporter. You join the inner circle for your monthly membership. You will get advance copies of publications, informative responses to your questions, and one-on-one workshops to help you overcome your obstacles.

## Conclusion

The willingness to develop and function on modifications is referred to in the agile project management approach. It's a strategy for dealing with and potentially surviving in a volatile world. Agile, according to the agile manifesto's authors, denotes adaptability and openness to transition. It's about teams finding out what's going on in the world, defining the sources of confusion, and figuring out how to adjust as they go. Agile is a software development and project management method that emphasizes continuous planning, learning, development, collaboration, evolutionary change, and early delivery. Its ultimate aim is to encourage people to be adaptable to transition. Agile allows teams to handle several tasks by splitting them down into phases and actively engaging cooperation partners. There is constant growth and iteration at any step. Agile enables a team to efficiently and reliably provide value to their clients. A team submits work in tiny, consumable increments rather than relying on a big bang start. Agile teams review requirements, strategies, and outcomes daily, implying that they have a system in place for easily adapting to change. While the conventional Waterfall approach required one person to commit to the whole project before passing it over to the next contributor or authority, Agile requires cross-functional teams to collaborate. Agile emphasizes flexibility, teamwork, confidence, and open communication among team members. Teams self–organize around small tasks and assignments to decide how they can accomplish the job, even though product owners or group leaders prescribe how it can be delivered.

CPSIA information can be obtained
at www.ICGtesting.com
Printed in the USA
BVHW090323220621
610126BV00011B/2175

9 781802 711189